COLLABORATIVE
SCHOOL LEADERSHIP
A CRITICAL GUIDE

Sara Miller McCune founded SAGE Publishing in 1965 to support the dissemination of usable knowledge and educate a global community. SAGE publishes more than 1000 journals and over 800 new books each year, spanning a wide range of subject areas. Our growing selection of library products includes archives, data, case studies and video. SAGE remains majority owned by our founder and after her lifetime will become owned by a charitable trust that secures the company's continued independence.

Los Angeles | London | New Delhi | Singapore | Washington DC | Melbourne

COLLABORATIVE
SCHOOL LEADERSHIP
A CRITICAL GUIDE

PHILIP A WOODS | AMANDA ROBERTS

Los Angeles | London | New Delhi
Singapore | Washington DC | Melbourne

Los Angeles | London | New Delhi
Singapore | Washington DC | Melbourne

SAGE Publications Ltd
1 Oliver's Yard
55 City Road
London EC1Y 1SP

SAGE Publications Inc.
2455 Teller Road
Thousand Oaks, California 91320

SAGE Publications India Pvt Ltd
B 1/I 1 Mohan Cooperative Industrial Area
Mathura Road
New Delhi 110 044

SAGE Publications Asia-Pacific Pte Ltd
3 Church Street
#10-04 Samsung Hub
Singapore 049483

© Philip A. Woods and Amanda Roberts 2018

First published 2018

Editor: James Clark
Assistant editor: Robert Patterson
Production editor: Tom Bedford
Copyeditor: Christine Bitten
Proofreader: Thea Watson
Indexer: Gary Kirby
Marketing manager: Dilhara Attygalle
Cover design: Sheila Tong
Typeset by: C&M Digitals (P) Ltd, Chennai, India
Printed in the UK

Library of Congress Control Number: 2017951046

British Library Cataloguing in Publication data

A catalogue record for this book is available from the British Library

ISBN 978-1-4739-8084-6
ISBN 978-1-4739-8085-3 (pbk)

At SAGE we take sustainability seriously. Most of our products are printed in the UK using FSC papers and boards. When we print overseas we ensure sustainable papers are used as measured by the PREPS grading system. We undertake an annual audit to monitor our sustainability.

CONTENTS

ABOUT THE AUTHORS

Professor PHILIP A. WOODS
Philip A. Woods is Director of the Centre for Educational Leadership and Professor of Educational Policy, Democracy and Leadership at the University of Hertfordshire, UK, as well as Immediate Past Chair of the British Educational Leadership, Management and Administration Society (BELMAS). His work focuses principally on leadership as a distributed and democratic process and on issues of governance, equity and change towards more democratic and holistic learning environments. He is author of over 130 publications and has wide-ranging experience and expertise in leading, managing and participating in major funded projects for organisations including the British Academy, UK government and European Union.

Dr AMANDA ROBERTS
Amanda Roberts is a Senior Lecturer in Learning and Teaching at the University of Hertfordshire, UK. Amanda's subject, pedagogic and professional knowledge has been developed through experience in a variety of educational roles, including leadership positions in four secondary schools culminating in headship. She subsequently formed a successful educational consultancy company, providing support for leadership and learning in a variety of contexts. Her work now focuses principally on leadership (including student leadership), coaching and curriculum development. In her current research she uses creative methodologies for exploring leadership experience and identity development.

PREFACE

What *is* leadership? What *should* leadership be? How these questions are answered has vital implications for leadership practice. The first invites us to identify critically important features about the nature of leadership. The second requires us to decide what is of greatest significance in defining the purpose and values of leadership practice and essential to making leadership worthwhile.

In response to the first question, there is much evidence that leadership is best conceived as a distributed, complex and emergent process, rather than simply a linear, top-down activity. Leadership is also an outcome of people's intentions, which embrace their creativity, blindspots, goodness and frailties. They give the human spark to leadership, as individuals and through shared intentions. Recognising this, we argue that leadership is the product both of intentionalities and emergence. Intentionality is the will, feelings and reflections that forge the intent to make a difference, with and through others. Emergence is the momentum and energy that arise from countless interactions between organisational members across and beyond an organisation. A consequence of leadership being emergent is that it is a process, whether we like it or not, that involves both non-positional and positional leadership – that is, those without and those with formal authority to act as a leader.

An implication of the answer to the first question – that leadership is a distributed phenomenon and the practice of leadership involves intentionality and emergence – is that all who contribute to leadership (in either non-positional or positional roles) need to work with this fact about the nature of leadership.

This claim about what leadership is says nothing in itself about the purpose and values of leadership. Yes, leadership is a distributed and complex process, but this can include all kinds of leadership styles and ethical aims. The complex processes and interactions that give rise to leadership may include directive and highly authoritarian styles, collaborative and participative styles, as well as transactional and other kinds of leadership practices.

The second question is equally important. The 'should' question has to be answered. In response to this necessity, our argument is that leadership practice needs to embrace an explicit commitment to holistically democratic and social justice values. Through this it nurtures a fundamental ethical good, which is relational freedom – that is, growth towards self-awareness and self-determination for the self and others, which might also be termed 'freedom with others'.

We elaborate the responses to the two questions in this book. These make up a philosophy or overarching view of leadership that is intended to inform the practice of leadership. This overarching view constitutes what we mean by collaborative leadership. It understands leadership as an emergent process in which the intentionality and actions of non-positional and positional leaders, as well as commitment to values of holistic democracy and social justice, are integral and explicit features of how leadership should be conceived and practised. Our conception of collaborative leadership does not prescribe one particular practice or style for all times and circumstances; rather it offers a framework for understanding leadership, for building a culture of collaboration and for reflecting critically on the decisions – small and large – that everyone who contributes to leadership makes through their intentions and actions. It is true that this view encourages or looks most kindly upon styles of leadership that are collaborative and participatory; a predisposition to such practice underpins the leadership. Nevertheless, we recognise too that the exigencies of everyday life may require at times different, more directive styles where these are justified as being necessary in the light of values such as social justice (e.g. to protect the vulnerable). A key point is that the explicit commitment to values of holistic democracy and social justice builds into the distributed concept of leadership an impetus to critical reflexivity. Individual and collective questioning of the extent to which leadership practice advances these values is inherent to the overarching view of leadership expounded in the book.

In summary, the book elaborates and illustrates two things. Firstly, leadership is a distributed, complex and emergent process in which the individual and collective intentionalities of non-positional and positional leaders are integral and active elements. A crucial implication is that it is important to recognise and work with this emergent and intentional nature of leadership. Secondly, leadership practice, to be worthwhile, needs to be framed within an explicit value-base in which leadership is committed to values of holistic democracy and social justice that underpin aspirations to relational freedom. Collaborative leadership is the product of the way we answer both the 'is' and 'should' questions.

1

Introduction

About this book

This book is fundamentally about freedom as an essential part and goal of educational leadership. It is about how educators and learners can act with autonomy and play an active part in leadership as an emergent process arising out of people's everyday actions and interactions. Education is not, of course, about providing the freedom for everyone to do exactly what they want. We are not referring to the hedonistic freedom of a completely unfettered, individualistic free will. We are referring instead to social or relational freedom, in which a person's awareness and critical reasoning enable a significant degree of self-direction as an individual and as a social being who has a felt sense of connection with groups and organisations such as a school, professional community, family, class and friendship groups (Woods, 2017a). Relational freedom entails both the self and others growing towards autonomy. A fundamental purpose of an educational system and its leadership, in our view, is to nurture the capabilities that support such relational freedom.

In a world in which talk of state steering and domination of education proliferates, this may seem a provocative or potentially naive intent. But this starting point is also a recognition that relational freedom is essential to widely shared commitments to ideals of social justice.

> Freedom is a necessary condition of justice. For what justice, including social justice, means and what we have to do in order to approximate it cannot be decreed in paternalistic fashion but can only be found through intensive democratic discussion. (Inaugural speech of Joachim Gauck, Federal President of Germany, 23 March 2012, quoted in Dallmayr, 2016: 136)

In addition, we argue that being guided by an ideal does not automatically mean that thinking and practice have to be unrealistic. Instead, it means fully understanding the underpinning values from which appropriate leadership intentions and actions can grow. It is this fundamental value-base that gives meaning to educational leadership and which we both advocate and seek to explore in this book. The term 'critical' in the book's sub-title refers to the central importance we give to an explicit, value-based framework, essential for the kind of questioning integral to leadership committed to relational freedom. We offer the book as a guide, a resource to support the critical thinking about leadership necessary to develop collaborative leadership practice.

This introduction would be quite different if we conformed to the definition of education offered by the standards agenda. In this case, the horizon of our ambition would be to focus on identifying and exploring ways in which schools could be supported in 'driving up' standards of attainment. This book is instead a testament to a broader view of educational purpose, one which seeks to understand how to support young people to develop the totality of capabilities which enable human flourishing. Such flourishing, we would argue, can only be achieved in a context in which freedom is recognised, nourished and championed. The exercise of such freedom involves agency which is not unreflexive and oppressively confined, but is characterised by questioning and an informed degree of self-determination. So, recognising work examining leadership and agency, such as Frost (2006) and Raelin (2016a), we explore how we might better understand the kind of agency (pro-active agency) associated with leadership committed to freedom.

One of the most influential developments in recent understandings of leadership is the growing appreciation of its distributed character and its emergence from a host of actions and interactions across organisations. This is well documented in reviews and accounts within and beyond education (for example, Bennett et al., 2003; Bolden, 2011; Fitzgerald et al., 2013; Gronn, 2002; Tian et al., 2016; Woods and Roberts, 2013a). The concept of leadership refers to the influences, arising from human intentions and actions, that make a difference to what a group or organisation does – its direction, goals, culture, practice – and how it is seen and experienced by those who work in or relate to the group or organisation. Appreciating the distributed character of leadership, we use the term 'leadership' to mean the practice of all who contribute to leadership both through individual and collective actions. This includes not only positional leaders, such as senior and middle leaders, but also non-positional leaders – namely, all those who, without possessing formal authority as a leader, use their agency to influence others and the school (its direction, goals, culture, practice), such as students, teachers, support staff and parents.

Within this discourse, many different labels are given to alternative approaches to leadership – distributed, shared, democratic and so on. Where we append a single adjective to the term 'leadership', we use the term 'collaborative', although it is not an adjectival label that we seek to promote above others.

The book is based on our experience of developing and researching non-positional leadership, together with our critical reading of discourses of leadership within and outside education that view leadership as emergent and distributed (e.g. eco-leadership, complexity theory and leadership-as-practice), and reviews and critiques of distributed leadership. It draws on our research on democratic leadership and distributed leadership for equity and learning (e.g. Roberts, 2011; Roberts and Nash, 2009; Roberts and Woods, 2017; Woods, 2005, 2011, 2015a/b, 2016a/b, 2017a/b; Woods and Roberts, 2016; Woods [G.J.] and Woods, 2008, 2013; Woods and Woods [G.J.], 2013; Woods et al., 2016), including our work in international projects investigating cases of school leadership and collaborative teacher learning (Roberts and Woods, 2017; Woods, 2015a; Woods et al., 2016).

The EU-funded projects include the European Policy Network on School Leadership (EPNoSL) (www.schoolleadership.eu) and the European Methodological Framework for Facilitating Teachers' Collaborative Learning (EFFeCT) project (http://oktataskepzes.tka.hu/en/effect-project).

Challenging prevailing leadership assumptions

The idea of leadership as a hierarchical phenomenon is a familiar one, most readily associated with people's experience. Here, leadership is seen as linear and as the source of power flowing down a pyramidical organisational structure. As Fink (2005: 102) puts it: 'instrumental leaders lead from the apex of a pyramid'. It envisages a top-down flow from policy formulation and decision-making to implementation, from the senior, positional leaders to the people who operationalise policy and decisions. From this perspective, leadership is what the boss or senior people in an organisation do. It is associated with decisions, instructions and guidance, cascading down a hierarchy of authority and power, with 'one fixed power centre at the zenith of the hierarchy' (Tian, 2015: 56).

Such a view not only offers a description of leadership in action but predicates this on a particular set of values. Hierarchy has a symbiotic relationship with the view that people are fundamentally dependent on being directed and provided with instructions and definitive guidance in order to know what to do. This viewpoint can be summarised as a philosophy of dependence (Woods, 2016a). Not everyone in rigidly hierarchical organisations embraces such a philosophy of dependence, although reliance on hierarchical leadership tends to cultivate it. At the centre of this philosophy lies a conviction that an elevated authority is necessary to show the majority the way to awareness, learning and right action. The task for followers is to make sure they are following the right leader who can make this choice of the right way. Reliance on a top-down, command-and-control type of leadership, where the 'heroic', charismatic leader is seen as the gold standard, is an unsurprising corollary of such a perspective.

Diverse ways of expressing and exploring the idea that leadership is not the exclusive province of the senior leader can be found in the discourse around shared leadership, eco-leadership and democratic leadership, in ideas such as leadership-as-practice and in work about the changing nature of organisations and leadership within them.[1] As Donna Ladkin (2010: 5) puts it, there is an emerging post-positivist conversation 'about ways of engaging rigorously with the leadership terrain'.

Heroic leadership has a long history. In pre-modern times, people tended to see the world as fixed according to a necessary, and rightful, hierarchy of authority – such as God, then King, then nobility and, finally, people. The philosopher Charles Taylor (2007: Chapter 4) suggests that a fundamental shift has taken place in modern society, where the underlying way of thinking is to see all social arrangements as contingent on the benefit they are deemed to bring. By this token, whether to have hierarchy, and how it should be formed and who should be recruited to which levels in it are matters for decision in the light of circumstances, values and perceived benefits. Conceiving of leadership as an emergent process is in this modern spirit of questioning organisational arrangements in search of better ways of leadership practice. A key argument for seeing leadership as a distributed phenomenon is that it is a more valid representation of actual leadership practice in organisations. This does not mean that dependence on or predispositions in favour of hierarchy have gone away. Arguably, an assumption of a primeval need for it remains strong in the modern imagination, as we discuss in Chapter 3.

Complexity theory, distributed leadership and decentred agency feed the discourse of leadership as an emergent phenomenon, questioning reliance on a

---

1 See Wang et al. (2014) on shared leadership, Western (2008, 2013) on eco-leadership, Woods (2005, 2015b) on democratic leadership, as well as Gratton (2004, 2007), and Raelin (2016b) on leadership-as-practice. Ulhøi and Müller (2014) map the 'landscape' of shared and distributed leadership.

hierarchical view of leadership (Bates, 2016; Caldwell, 2006, 2007; Griffin, 2002; Harris and DeFlaminis, 2016; Stacey, 2012). From this viewpoint, numerous organisational actors initiate, influence and co-create change, the outcome of which forges the character and direction of the organisation. Complexity theory has introduced a new and keen appreciation of the uncertainty that characterises the complicated and ongoing interactions that make up organisations, including schools (Boulton et al., 2015; Hawkins and James, 2017). It has also explored the implications of such an organisational view for leadership (Bates, 2016; Flinn and Mowles, 2014; Griffin, 2002; Stacey, 2012). Individuals are unable to plan the actions of others and the myriad of interactions between the plans and actions of others, and so they cannot 'plan and control population-wide "outcomes"' (Stacey, 2012: 18). Decisions by a senior leader or a senior leadership team are mediated and interpreted by people across the organisation, who themselves may initiate changes as they go about their everyday practice. Viewing leadership as emergent is often associated with questioning the all-knowing character of single or elite, heroic leaders and the legitimacy of seeing them as the exclusive fount of good leadership.

This discourse of leadership as complex, emergent and distributed is having widespread influence in thinking about leadership and its development in many organisations and sectors, including public services such as education and health (West et al., 2015), and in numerous countries, such as the US and China, as well as the UK, Finland and other parts of Europe.[2] Such attention to leadership as distributed and emergent has led to advances in understanding and practice. There remain, however, serious limitations in the current field, to which we make brief reference in the section which follows and in more detail in Chapter 3. A key purpose of this book is to maintain what is valuable in the idea of distributed leadership, to address its limitations and to give a boost to widening educational leadership's horizon of ambition so that it embraces the fundamental educational aim of nurturing relational freedom.

The promise of distributed leadership

Distributed leadership appears to promise an alternative to the unjust power differences and inequalities that condition effective participation in leadership. However, the field of distributed leadership has itself yet to convincingly address these issues. Even where it is believed that leadership is or should be distributed,

---

2 In the UK examples of attention to the practice of distributed leadership are apparent in the work of the RSA (Hallgarten et al., 2016) and the National College for School Leadership (Woods and Roberts, 2013a). Examples in the US include DeFlaminis et al. (2016) and, in Finland and China, Tian (2015, 2016). Evidence of European interest is in Kollias and Hatzopoulos (2013) and Woods (2015a).

in practice traditional hierarchies of formal authority, with people occupying senior leadership positions, endure in most organisations. Many studies recognise this of course, and there have been attempts to conceptually capture the practical co-mingling of senior leadership relations and distributed leadership, in the notion of hybrid leadership, for example. Some exploration of the different forms of authority has also been undertaken.[3] However, more needs to be done to integrate an understanding of asymmetrical relationships into a conceptualisation of leadership as distributed and emergent. An inadequate hybridisation is likely to fuel Jacky Lumby's allegation that hybridisation is simply 'a get-out clause for those needing to justify their adherence to [distributed leadership]' (Lumby, 2016: 12).

In some respects, Lumby is right: there are limitations in the way that distributed leadership is often understood and practised (Woods and Woods [G.J.], 2013), and it takes many forms (Gronn, 2002; Tian et al., 2016). However, we would argue that this 'hybridisation' (Lumby, 2016: 164) is not a clever device to deflect criticism but instead results from authentic attempts to understand leadership complexity in order to mine its potential to support school improvement and student learning. Peter Gronn concludes that distributed leadership 'provides merely part of the story of what goes on in educational organisations' (Gronn, 2016: 169). Our view is that the proper response to the impetus of criticism is therefore to ask: how do we better deploy and develop the concept of distributed leadership, and our understanding of the wider practice of leadership distribution (Chapter 2) within which it sits, so that its value in illuminating practice is realised? Our intention is to suggest how such a question may be addressed through offering two propositions about leadership. These are briefly introduced in the two sections which follow, before being discussed in more detail in Chapters 4 and 5.

Our first proposition: Intentionality and emergence

The first proposition is that we need to see leadership through two lenses,[4] intentionality and emergence, which then allow us to explore issues of agency and power and the complexities of change. Leadership is not a 'thing' in itself, hence

---

3 See Day et al. (2009) and Gronn (2009) on hybrid leadership, and Woods (2016b) on authority, power and distributed leadership.

4 By using the term 'lens' we are highlighting how the concepts used in the propositions enable us to see and understand different aspects of the phenomenon of leadership. This is what concepts do. They provide an approximate account (perpetually provisional, subject to continuing research) of what some aspect of the world is like. In using the term 'lens' we are highlighting that our propositions and concepts are the result of a choice (a reasoned and plausible one, we would argue). The term 'lens' is not meant to imply that those lenses can merely be adopted or discarded at will without argument or evidence.

there are difficulties in seeking to define it conclusively. It is helpful to think about leadership as encapsulating a relationship between two kinds of phenomena leading to purposeful, if not straightforwardly predictable, influence and change in societies and organisations.[5]

The first, intentionality, is the will or intention to make a difference, with and through others, which leads to action. As agents of action, people express meaning, purpose and goals. This is true in whatever way or at whatever level the person contributes to leadership – whether as a non-positional or positional leader, for example. The 'genesis of human actions' lies 'in the reasons, intentions and plans of human beings' (Bhaskar, 2010: 62). Intentionality is this genesis – that is, the concerns, purposes, deliberations and awareness of the potential for agency that lead to a person doing something. In leadership, intentionality gives rise to doing things that influence the group or organisation – its direction, its goals and culture, and its practice.

A basic sociological proposition about people's agency is that individuals engage in continual reflexivity and have the 'power to deliberate internally upon what to do in situations that were not of their making' (Archer, 2003: 342). This proposition is important because it highlights the fact that an individual's capacity for conscious initiation of action is not submerged and lost in the distributed and emergent process of leadership. Instead, it is an integral part of it. Whilst we recognise the value, indeed the necessity, of the perspective that is 'concerned with how leadership emerges and unfolds' through the everyday practices of interacting organisational members (Raelin, 2016a: 3), we want to underline the importance of also retaining a focus on individuals and their agency. This is crucial to our argument that intentionality, and the effects of intentionality, infuse distributed processes of leadership.

The capacity of individuals and groups for conscious and influential intentionality varies. One factor affecting this is the context in which people are placed. Opportunities are needed in that context for intentionality to be turned into action. Numerous internal factors affect the degree to which a person or group may feel able to formulate independent ideas and plans. These include feelings of confidence, assumptions of what is possible and the information and knowledge they have access to, which all impinge on capacity for conscious and creative intentionality.

The second lens, emergence, is the perpetual process of complex interactions in which intentionalities and their consequent actions take place and which they become part of.

Ralph Stacey (2012) turned to the sciences of uncertainty and complexity to develop an understanding of the turbulent context in which leadership occurs.

---

5   The account in this paragraph of leadership as not a thing in itself but a way of talking about a relationship between two aspects is in part informed by reading William James' (2004) discussion of consciousness.

He uses complexity theory to suggest that the features and outcomes of organisational life emerge from a mass of human interactions, a radically different picture, as we noted earlier, to the common, linear, hierarchical view of leadership in which powerful organisational leaders enforce strategic plans, underpinned by their own value systems. Emergence – that is, the ongoing interactions and their effects that constitute leadership processes – is at the heart of an understanding of leadership as distributed and complex.

Complexity theory highlights the way in which intentions do not necessarily, or even often, lead to the planned end; and they certainly do not do so in a neat, linear process of cause and effect. The detail and sweep of organisational life – both stability and change – arise from the perpetual interplay of people, ideas, social structures, artefacts, environmental conditions and relationships. Outcomes are unplanned, in the sense that they arise as the result of countless variables which intervene during the interplays that constitute organisational life and are thus beyond detailed monitoring and control. Intentions are interpreted, changed and fashioned during these ongoing interplays.

The sociologist Margaret Archer honed the argument that social life is an emergent process in order to identify the essential character of emergence – namely, the interplay of the people (whose dispositions, motivations, intentions and actions constitute agency) and the parts (social structures).[6] This elemental understanding enables the examination of social stability and change. The interplay of people and parts can be studied to understand or illuminate why a society or an organisation is like this rather than like that – to explore 'why matters are so and not otherwise' (Archer, 1995: 167). In other words, there are patterns and continuities in organisational life and outcomes. Some actors are more influential and powerful than others in sustaining or disrupting these patterns and continuities whilst some structures are more constraining than others. However, as discussed above, intentionality, by opening the possibilities for difference, change and innovation, demonstrates that people are not wholly determined. Emergence embraces both continuity *and* change; it helps us understand '*both* the regular patterning of wants in different parts of society *and* ... the personal differences which ... make actions something quite different from mechanical responses to hydraulic [societal] pressures' (Archer, 1995: 132).

From the discussion so far, it is clear that intentionality and emergence occur simultaneously. They are intertwined, or, to put it another way, intentionality is

---

6 See for example discussions in Archer (1995) on pages 15, 63, and Chapter 3. The concept of 'people', the creators of agency, denotes individuals who are each characterised by a stratified set of features according to Archer's analysis – actor, agent, person. The individual is an actor (an occupant of social roles) whose access to such roles is shaped by their being an agent (a member of social groups, such as a gender type or social class), and both of these roles as actor and agent are anchored in the individual's condition as a person with capacities common to being human. See Archer, 1995: 255–256.

embedded in the process of emergence. Agency (people) and structures (the parts) interact with each other. People exist within social structures by which they are shaped and which they, in turn, mediate. From this position, people give rise to intentions which they go on to live out through actions and practices, which in turn sustain or change those social structures, constituting a perpetual trialectic process, involving the person (who engages in intentionality), action and structure (Woods, 2016a). Intentionality and emergence are put forward as two lenses, not because they denote separate entities but because, for the purpose of understanding and practising leadership, we need to ensure that the intentional individual is not subsumed and lost within emergence.

Our second proposition: Integrating a philosophy of co-development

Our second proposition is that that a social justice and democratic values position, encompassed within what we term a philosophy of co-development (Woods, 2016a), needs to be integrated into the dual perspective on leadership discussed above. We refer to this as a *philosophy* of co-development – and similarly to its contrasting position as a *philosophy* of dependence – because the term 'philosophy' for us denotes a fundamental orientating position concerning the nature of human beings. These very different philosophies each describe a viewpoint on what people are capable of and what is of value and ethically preferable.

Leadership as a practice that impacts upon people and the environment inherently involves the expression of values or ethical priorities, either explicitly or implicitly, through that practice. Any understanding of leadership therefore has to be critically examined from the perspective of the values it promotes or implies. The approach to leadership we are advocating has a clear ethical orientation grounded in a specified value-base. In this section we consider the kind of ethical orientation to others that is most important and indicate how our second proposition is a response to one of the weaknesses in the field of distributed leadership.

Aristotle provides a useful conceptual typology for reflecting on what we consider to be most worthwhile. Three types of friendship are proposed by Aristotle, which can be utilised to explore the different purposes and reasons that may underlie the *philia* – the affinity, liking, mutual affection – in positive and valued relationships. These types have been examined and used by Stockwell et al. (2017) in the investigation of educational partnerships and they can help to clarify for our purpose what kind of ethical orientation best supports good education and good living.

The functional or utility-based relationship is one where the chief source of that *philia* is the gain that each party derives from it. A contractual arrangement is an example of such a functional or utility-based relationship, where there is an exchange, such as money for goods or a service. The pleasure-based relationship is where the chief value is the enjoyment, delight and positive feelings that each of the parties finds through the relationship. The gain from the pleasure-based relationship, and hence its felt value, is affective or aesthetic gratification that comes to each party.

The third type – the virtuous relationship – is where the parties value the enhancement of virtues and ethical growth that occur through their shared activities and interconnection. In the virtuous partnership, the source of *philia* between the parties is not benefits such as gain or pleasure which are external or incidental to the person with whom one is in relation; rather, it is the flourishing as human beings that the parties to the relationship experience and that occur as they share important parts of their lives. The partners value each other for who they are, and they value the relationship for its nourishment in each of them of intrinsically worthwhile virtues such as fair-mindedness, care, patience, diligence, courage, temperance, wisdom, honesty and integrity.[7]

We see an ethical orientation which prioritises the value of the third type of relationship, the virtuous relationship, as vital to good education and good living. It follows, therefore, that the flourishing of human beings and the nurturing of ethical sensibilities integral to that flourishing should be the paramount aim of leadership. The assumption underlying such philosophical reflections is that people are capable of some degree of choice and self-directed agency. The enhancement of freedom and a sense of empowered agency – that is, increasing the degree of control over actions and their consequences[8] – is an ethical aim of fostering leadership as a shared and distributed process. As we emphasised at the outset of this chapter, we are not referring here to individualistic freedom and the idea of 'freedom from' – the absence of all restraints and obstacles so that the person is free to do whatever they like. We are referring to relational freedom and what can be called 'freedom with' – the capability, nurtured with and through others, to shape one's character and actions in ways that help the self and others flourish (Woods, 2017a).

To date, the field of distributed leadership has insufficiently addressed this question of values and where it places itself. Much of the field is framed within school effectiveness and improvement concerns that are associated with dominant policy

---

7 Carr (2011: 175–176) provides an interesting analysis of pedagogical virtues in teaching which illustrates the range and nature of virtues. These comprise intellectual virtues (such as intellectual honesty, integrity, scrupulousness, persistence, open-mindedness, fair-mindedness, accuracy), procedural virtues (such as care, patience, attention to detail, application, industry, diligence), and moral virtues (such as courage, temperance 'in order to act in a calm, patient and controlled way under stress or provocation', wisdom, honesty, integrity and 'above all … justice to be and to be perceived by pupils as fair').

8 For a discussion in the field of psychology, see Moore (2016).

priorities, giving rise to the critique that distributed leadership has been harnessed to marketising and performative agendas that narrow educational purpose (for example, Hall et al., 2013; Hammersley-Fletcher and Strain, 2011; Woods and Woods [G.J.], 2013). This is not to say that researchers in these fields lack values,[9] but it is to observe that the formulation of a robust and challenging ethical stance and policy critique is not usually seen as a necessary component of this approach. We judge the idea of distributed leadership as weakened by this absence of a radical, conceptual orientation to social justice and inclusion.

Founding our conceptualisation of leadership on a philosophy of co-development (Woods, 2016a) addresses this weakness through encompassing the ideas of holistic democracy and an expansive view of social justice. From this philosophical perspective, we learn and work best collaboratively, bringing together the different experiences, expertise and ideas as diverse people in a group or organisation. An underlying commitment to social justice and a rich conception of democratic values underpins effective mutual support of this kind.

The notion of holistic democracy places value on both meaning and participation (Woods, 2011; Woods and Woods, 2012; Woods and Woods [G.J.], 2013). It is about enabling people to be co-creators of their social environment and, through this, make the most of their innate capacity to learn and develop their highest capabilities and ethical sensibilities and to feel a meaningful connection with the world they live in. Central to the practice of holistic democracy, therefore, is the opportunity for people to grow as whole persons, able to evolve a meaningful life for themselves and with others. To create opportunities for such growth, the facilitation of participation should be based on principles of mutual respect, critical dialogue, independent thinking and a sense of belonging and connectedness (in the group, community, organisation and the wider human and natural world).

Bound up with holistic democratic practice is an expansive notion of social justice. This interrelates with principles of holistic democracy and spans four dimensions. The dimensions are concerned with the fair distribution of respect, participation, development opportunities (that is, the opportunity to learn and grow as a person with a capacity for independent thinking and connectedness with others) and resources (including the material supports of learning such as IT, books and digital resources) (Woods, 2012; Woods and Roberts, 2013a).

Leadership founded on a philosophy of co-development integrates into its conceptualisation these values of holistic democracy and social justice. An unmistakable ethical commitment is thus, crucially, built into the notion of leadership – a commitment to a set of values that leadership should be aiming to realise. This specificity provides a framework for critical reflection on leadership practice.

---

9 Researchers such as DeFlaminis et al. (2016) and Harris (2012) for example, are committed to enhancing leaning and educational achievement and reducing inequalities in attainment.

Structure of this book

Research giving insight into potential benefits and factors that are conducive to leadership distribution working well is discussed in Chapter 2, whilst in Chapter 3 challenges and critiques are considered. These include difficulties in the conceptualisation of distributed leadership as well as critiques of the purpose and use of distributed leadership. Critiques concern the extent to which distributed leadership serves economistic and performative aims, promotes learning confined by a constricted view of what it means to grow and flourish as a person and fails to address unjust power differences and relational inequalities that condition effective involvement in leadership. These questions surface issues of acute importance to attempts to improve leadership by enhancing the awareness and practice of leadership distribution.

Chapters 4 and 5 are pivotal. Mindful of the benefits and challenges of leadership distribution identified in the previous two chapters, we articulate in these chapters our conception of collaborative leadership that is intended to maintain what is valuable in the idea of distributed leadership and address its limitations. This conception is founded on the two propositions about leadership introduced above. The first of these, explained in Chapter 4, concerns intentionality and emergence and helps in exploring both issues of agency and power on the one hand and the complexities of change on the other. The second, explained in Chapter 5, concerns the necessity of integrating core critical values into this dual perspective, articulated for us through a philosophy of co-development. Chapter 5 explains the constituent ideas of holistic democracy and social justice, and argues that a particular kind of intentionality – critical intentionality – is integral to relational freedom and pro-active agency.

This leads us to Chapters 6 and 7 in which the intimate relationship between leadership and learning is explored. In Chapter 6 we emphasise the importance of understanding leadership as a process that inherently involves learning. We then argue that collaborative leadership is a reciprocal learning process that is discursively and collectively created by the leadership population across the school – by both non-positional and positional leaders. People who are engaged in collaborative leadership are contributing to and facilitating each other's learning. With the philosophy of co-development as a value-base, the practice of reciprocal learning aims to enhance freedom and involves ethical reflexivity and learning.

Chapter 7 turns to the day-to-day operation of leadership as a reciprocal learning process and presents its essential principles as a learning model of change that supports the growth of collaborative leadership in schools. The learning model brings to the fore the importance of critically reflexive personal self-activity as part of collaborative learning and the centrality of the values of co-development which encourage questioning of who might be marginalised or excluded in processes of leadership development.

The remaining chapters of the book explore implications for the development of collaborative leadership. Chapter 8 explores the structures and emergent spaces that facilitate learning and critical intentionality. It considers how we might make sense of the complex interplays that are characteristic of emergence. Rather than attempting to provide a blueprint for change which would run counter to the cautionary insights of complexity theory, it offers an overview, to inform change in schools or other settings, of interacting structures and spaces that help to promote collaborative leadership. The chapter sets out the kind of structures and their specific characters that are likely to enable collaborative leadership: a participatory culture, enabling institutional architecture and an open social environment. It also recognises the importance of internal processes of the subjective spaces in people and how these are affected by the kinds of outer supports, including socially constructed free spaces, available to help facilitate critical reflexivity and pro-active agency.

Chapters 9 and 10 are about change and the development of collaborative leadership, with an emphasis in Chapter 9 on change from across the school and in Chapter 10 on identity change. Chapter 9 considers challenges inherent in the role of senior, positional leaders in seeking to develop the role of both non-positional and positional leadership in advancing collaborative leadership. It argues that it is essential to make a fundamental shift beyond a primary focus on the senior leader granting or supporting a collaborative leadership culture or delegating responsibilities: leadership development and change should focus on leadership as a pedagogical, reciprocal learning process which involves actions and interactions by a range of organisational members in non-positional and positional leadership roles across a school leadership landscape.

Chapter 10 recognises that collaborative leadership practice involves changes in how those in both non-positional and positional leadership roles see themselves and the kinds of attitudes and capabilities they see as important for them to foster and develop, and that these changes have an impact on identity. Four practices are discussed that we suggest are integral to leadership development for collaborative leadership and are constituent elements of ongoing identity change: clarifying values, reframing leadership, nurturing of key capabilities and the construction of identity as a shared and collective process. As a support to critical reflexivity, questions framed by the values of holistic democracy are offered towards the close of the chapter.

Chapter 11 draws together key ideas presented in the book and uses them as a basis for a series of catalysts for reflection and action offered in the chapter. The catalysts comprise questions that can be used or adapted by both individuals and teams. They are designed to help facilitate values clarification, leadership reframing, and evaluation – through comparative reflections on practices associated with 'dependence' and 'co-development' – of priorities and progress in developing collaborative leadership.

2

Benefits of Leadership Distribution

Introduction

This chapter discusses what we can glean from research about leadership distribution and the conditions in which it appears to work well. Leadership distribution for our purposes refers to the practice of leadership activities being undertaken by those in non-positional roles as well as by positional leaders; the extension and support of such practice may be the object of deliberate policy (by a school, say), but need not be. Leadership distribution may be identified according to different terms in research and by practitioners – such as distributed leadership, shared leadership or some other label. We draw in this discussion from research that uses different or no specific labels for leadership distribution.

It is difficult to identify the effects of a complex process like leadership distribution in organisations that are affected by a variety of factors and changes. Complexity theory encourages us not to interpret in a linear fashion the effects of a single source of change, let alone a more diffuse source that is represented by the practice of leadership distribution. In addition to this, it has to be recognised that research relevant to understanding leadership distribution does not necessarily focus exclusively on the concept of distributed leadership since much research into leadership 'implicitly, if not explicitly, takes a distributed perspective on leadership' (Timperley and Robertson, 2011: 6). It is possible, nevertheless, to conclude from research findings that there is evidence that leadership distribution, in the right conditions which we discuss below, can have beneficial effects.[1]

A large-scale study by Karen Seashore Louis et al. (2010: 13), for example, emphasised that to understand leadership it is essential to recognise the 'remarkable array of people who exercise formal or informal leadership in schools' and outside schools, and the 'web of interaction created by these sources' (Louis et al., 2010: 13). A theme that runs through much of the research and experience of leadership distribution is the impact it has on people and relationships. Where it works well, leadership distribution enhances the kind of relational freedom we refer to in Chapters 1 and 5 – that is, 'freedom with others': the capability, nurtured with and through others, to shape one's character and actions in ways that help the self and others flourish. At its best, leadership distribution nurtures and enhances people's sense of agency in this way.

Research on private companies and other organisations globally suggests that when 'we grow and develop, and we become innovative, energised and stimulated' and work co-operatively, 'we are able to create the positive energy that gives us joy and adds value to our companies' (Gratton, 2007: xi). Such research directly challenges the idea that commanding and controlling others is the best way to run an organisation. Where organisations are creative and working well, 'rather than be commanded, employees choose to develop important relationships with others, and rather than be controlled, they actively choose to make their time available to [a] collective sense of purpose' (Gratton, 2007: 46).

The discussion below draws on a range of published qualitative and quantitative research. It is structured according to three challenges that we see as of central concern to schools: to sustain learning, to be innovative in responding to contemporary opportunities and problems, and to foster democratic citizenship. The chapter concludes with a discussion of factors conducive to leadership distribution being beneficial.

---

1   Reviews of research on distributed leadership, and related concepts such as shared leadership, in education and other fields, include Bennett et al. (2003), Bolden (2011), Bolden et al. (2015), Fitzgerald et al. (2013), Thorpe et al. (2011), Tian et al. (2016), Ulhøi and Müller (2014), Wang et al. (2014), Woods and Roberts (2013a), and Woods et al. (2004).

Learning

Much of the pressure on schools is due to the standards and accountability agenda which focuses on improving measurable achievement. Such pressure is increasing significantly in school systems. As a result, intense pressure is placed on those who make, implement and interpret policy at all levels of these systems. International assessments such as PISA (Programme for International Student Assessment) increase pressure on politicians and civil servants in national ministries, who subsequently feel the need to make sure that schools are held accountable for students' learning and achievement. Those at regional and the middle levels of national education systems then experience the pressures of being held to account and being responsible for the success of their schools. School leaders, teachers and other staff – as well as students and parents – feel the force of national and regional expectations and interpret policy on the ground, translating it into everyday practice (Ward et al., 2016).

The real challenge for schools in relation to learning is more complex than the standards and accountability agenda, however. Learning is not equivalent to measurable achievement through tests and examinations. The challenge for schools is to enable learning that is deep and promotes the growth of the whole person. As we argue in Chapter 5, our view of educational leadership entails a commitment to holistic growth. Learning framed in this way develops cognitive and emotional abilities, skills for employment, ethical, aesthetic and spiritual capabilities, an understanding of democratic citizenship and appreciation of values such as justice and tolerance, as well as fostering the ability to reflect and learn continually throughout life.

Caution is needed in relation to 'evidence of any effects of distributed leadership on learning, as linkages are complex and the research on distributed leadership is diverse and comes from differing positions and paradigms' (Woods and Woods [G.J.], 2013: 4). Meng Tian et al. (2016: 154) reviewed research on distributed leadership between 2002 and 2013 and recognised in studies they examined the difficulty of 'modelling the causal relationship between distributed leadership and student learning outcomes, and the problem of generalising the identified applications of distributed leadership at the macro-level'. It is therefore important to recognise the dynamic and complex interplay between the personal (individual capabilities and development) and the structural, the latter involving, *inter alia*, development of institutional systems and a cultural climate that enable interpretation (autonomy) and a shared sense of direction (collectivity) (Woods [G.J.] and Woods, 2008).

Studies of the influence of leadership distribution on learning also have to consider how they should conceptualise and assess learning. Different approaches are apparent. For example, in the US study by Louis et al. (2010: 11), scores were used: 'we obtained student achievement data for literacy and mathematics in elementary and secondary grades, using scores on the states' tests for measuring Adequate Yearly Progress'. A study by Christopher Day et al. (2009) investigated leadership of improvement through a combination of statistical analyses of data sets on students' attainment and surveys of students on matters such as social and affective outcomes, relationships in schools and student engagement.[2] In our view, indicators of factors important to securing a beneficial outcome from the enhancement of leadership distribution can be gleaned from different kinds of studies using varied forms of outcome measurement, investigating different approaches to leadership distribution. Rather than enabling the construction of a linear model of cause-and-effect change, the results of such studies provide pointers to the conditions and actions that can play a part in connecting leadership distribution to learning. It is in that spirit that we approach the discussion of research on leadership distribution.

It is important to acknowledge that not all research shows a consistent pattern of effect in relation to the results of leadership distribution. For example, a US study, using school performance data (student results and school ratings on state mandated tests over time) found no consistent trends upward or downward in student performance in the schools studied (Anderson et al., 2009: 114). The authors concluded that from their study it is difficult 'to associate specific leadership distribution patterns and the principal's leadership role with higher or lower student performance, or with improving or declining performance' (Anderson et al., 2009: 131). They suggest that it may be more fruitful to research the relationship between leadership distribution and 'professional community' (Anderson et al., 2009: 132).

On the other hand, a four-year longitudinal study by Ronald Heck and Philip Hallinger (2010) produced results that suggest that leadership distribution can have important effects on student learning. It examined the effects of changing distributed leadership patterns on school improvement capacity and growth in

---

2 Day et al. (2009) explain: 'Through a combination of statistical analysis of national data sets on pupils' attainment three groups of schools were identified, all of which had made sustained improvements in academic outcomes but from different starting points': 'The analyses were based on relevant published data and key indicators (both value added measures that investigate pupil progress and raw indicators such as the percentage of pupils achieving performance benchmarks, e.g. level 4 at Key Stage 2, or 5 A*–C grades at GCSE at Key Stage 4)' (pp. 1, 18). This was supplemented by a student survey: 'In addition to the collection and analysis of pupils' cognitive outcomes (from Key Stage national assessment tests and GCSE results) a questionnaire was administered to approximately 30 pupils in each of the case study schools in year 6 (primary) and year 9 (secondary). This was informed by the initial review of literature and reviews of previous pupil survey instruments e.g. PISA..., RAPA... projects. The instrument provided: examples of social and affective outcomes of pupil learning; evidence of the relationships between leadership and pupils' perceptions of school and classroom climate; evidence of the relationships between leadership and pupils' perceptions of school and classroom conditions; and evidence of student engagement and identification with school.' (pp. 18, 19).

student learning in 197 primary schools in the US. The study found, *inter alia*, that distributed leadership was significantly related to improvement capacity and that distributed leadership had significant indirect effects on learning outcomes (through, for example, building the school's professional capacity and by maintaining a focus on improvements in teaching and learning). The measure of learning for the study was students' scores in maths and reading.

The study by Christopher Day et al. (2009: 110) identified, from extensive interview data collected on visits to 20 case study schools, a number of themes shown to have a positive impact on student outcomes. This included the distribution of leadership. The paragraph summarising the study's conclusion on this is worth quoting in full. It not only indicates the positive association with student outcomes, but also illustrates how distributing leadership is not the simple application of a single leadership form; rather, it is a process over time that involves diverse elements that contribute to what is summarised for convenience as distributed leadership (Day et al., 2009: 115).

> The heads purposively and progressively redesigned organisational structures and redefined and distributed more widely leadership and management responsibilities in order to promote greater staff engagement and ownership, and, through this, greater opportunities for student learning. While the exact nature of the re-structuring, change in roles and responsibilities and timing varied from school to school, there was a consistent pattern across schools of changing the existing hierarchy which included changing from a horizontal to a vertical structure, using TLRs [Teaching and Learning Responsibility payments], using ASTs [Advanced Skills Teachers] and the wider use of support staff. Lines of communication and responsibility were improved and new leadership and management responsibilities were clearly outlined. These were clear to all staff and allocated on the basis of ability along with recognition of people's strengths and organisational needs.

A different kind of project – the international Carpe Vitam Leadership for Learning research project involving academics and practitioners – also illustrates the positive outcomes of shared leadership, defined as the process by which 'people without formal status in their institutions were able to assume leadership roles' (Waterhouse, 2008: 369). The project aimed not simply to produce insights and recommendations but to develop a set of practical and intellectual tools, such as principles for practice and practical tools and instruments, designed to support organisational discourse and learning. Feedback on the development and use of these tools as the project progressed indicated the positive impact which the shared leadership they promoted had on fostering student social, emotional and cognitive learning.

There is substantial evidence that student leadership and active participation are associated with enhanced, more positive learning (Frost and Roberts, 2011). In the Leadership for Learning project, as well as teachers and others, shared leadership involved students (Frost et al., 2008: 5).

The inclusion of young people within distributed leadership was a major theme in the ... project. In some schools student leadership was fostered through the allocation of special roles such as being a mentor to younger students or as a representative on the school council. In some cases it was evident that student leadership opportunities arose where there had been a cultural shift caused by a more systemic focus on learning. This tended to create a virtuous circle of increased pupil attendance, greater student engagement, and more opportunities for authentic learning.

One of the conclusions apparent from many studies is that the impact of distributing leadership, where it works well, is on learning throughout the school – amongst teachers and senior leaders, as well as students – and on the conditions that help foster such learning. Studies show that teacher leadership and collaborative enquiry by teachers promote professional development and new knowledge, with benefits for teachers' and students' learning (Cameron et al., 2011; Frost, 2008; Holden, 2008). John DeFlaminis and colleagues assessed a 10-year programme which aimed to develop distributed leadership in schools in Pennsylvania, US, through the creation of teacher leaders and distributed leadership teams. They concluded that one of the clear benefits was improvement in teachers' instructional practice to address students' learning needs. They cite as an example the account of one school principal about a distributed leadership team (DeFlaminis et al., 2016: 34).

The professional development sessions are moving along quite well. Our conversations are more focus [sic] and directed to outcomes to support student achievement ... Teachers are more open to sharing and supporting their instructional practices and strategies with colleagues. The meetings are now a part of the school ...

Distribution of leadership, and related factors such as a collaborative culture amongst teachers, is an important part of effective leadership (Day et al., 2009: 186). Schools enacting democratic principles – such as shared intentional direction (developed collaboratively) and a participative approach to leadership – are more likely to foster greater professional learning amongst teachers (Kensler, 2008). A review of studies of teacher collaboration by Vangrieken et al. (2015: 27) found reported benefits for students and teachers. For example, there were reported improvements in students' 'understanding and performance' and positive impacts on such factors as teachers' skills and pedagogical strategies.

The cumulating research evidence would seem to suggest that, taking into account the complexities of research, there are positive associations between leadership distribution and both students' and professional learning. Indeed, leadership that is developed in a distributed and more democratic way can promote multilevel learning, at the student, staff, school and system levels (Frost, 2008).

It is helpful to consider one of the schools studied by Day and colleagues in order to illustrate the complexity of interaction, the importance of change over time and the need to understand distributed leadership in the context of other organisational factors and changes. The case is Eyhampton High School, an improving school at the time, in the UK. It is not presented by the study's researchers as a model of leadership change which is to be followed, but as a description of an example of change which involved introducing distributed leadership (Day et al., 2009: 166–181).

Many of the changes and the factors featured are only understandable in the specific context. For example, imposing tighter discipline in the school was seen as essential as one of the first changes because of the perceived indiscipline amongst students. The change in the school's modes of leadership went through phases over time in the school (see Figure 2.1). There was a phase of redesign, followed by rebuilding which included a focus on coaching and support and strengthening of care and mentoring for students; then reflection in which decision-making became more collegiate, learning more student-centred and a new curriculum introduced for diverse needs; with latterly the phase of distributed leadership which included dispersed responsibility, enhanced support for students and inclusion and a broadening of the curriculum for personal development.

Any positive effects of leadership distribution are not automatic. We discuss factors important in ensuring that leadership distribution has a positive impact

redesign	rebuilding	reflection	distributed leadership
autocratic leadership	performance management; coaching and support	some distribution, e.g. dispersing responsibility for observation; collegiate decision-making	responsibility dispersed to middle leaders, other staff, e.g. staff leading staff meeting, heads of department having more responsibility for running their departments, staff encouraged to innovative and create solutions
organising roles, responsibilities	peer observation		
vision, principles	raised expectations	more student-centred learning; students responsible for own learning	
professional development for all; mutual learning and support	targets for students		
greater support	strengthening of care and mentoring for students	new curriculum – flexible to meet diverse needs	support further enhanced for students and inclusion, using non-teaching staff
greater discipline	student voice	positive, friendly ethos, and high expectations	broadening curriculum to enhance personal development

Figure 2.1 Phases of leadership change at Eyhampton High School (adapted from Day et al., 2009: 168)

later in this chapter. In the meantime, we conclude that, where leadership distribution works well, it increases capacity – that is, more people at all levels are actively engaged in improving learning and more people are involved in improving their knowledge, capabilities and skills. Leadership distribution means that the leadership capabilities of staff and students not in senior, positional leadership roles are recognised and developed and, through people's own critical reflexivity and activity, can be unfettered to improve learning. In this way, it acts as a way to develop leadership capacity. Collaborative learning is facilitated, enabling people to work together and to share experience and ideas; and research indicates that co-operative learning, where it is organised well, is a highly effective form of learning (Slavin, 2010). Moreover, engagement and motivation are higher where leadership distribution works well. Staff and students are more enthusiastic and committed to the school and the activities undertaken to achieve its core purpose.

Innovation

Schools are expected to be innovative as organisations and to educate students so they will become the creators and innovators of the future. Promoting creativity and innovation is a driving aim on the policy agendas of nations and global bodies. The OECD (Organisation for Economic Co-operation and Development) succinctly expresses its view, underpinning a substantial international project on innovative learning environments, that, 'Innovation is a key element of today's societies and economies, and that includes how we learn' (OECD, 2013: 11). This results in the second challenge for schools, that is, high expectations to innovate.

A discourse of innovation and entrepreneurialism is a prominent dimension of performative governance, much of it informed by the assumptions of individualistic enterprise promoted by instrumentalising trends. The market as a competitive arena of struggle, as well as market-like environments in the public area, values the skills of innovators and entrepreneurs as means to achieving performative and financial goals. Yet, research and practice concerning innovation suggest that individualistic behaviour (by individuals and organisations) is not conducive to innovation. Collaboration is understood as integral to creating innovative cultures in all kinds of organisation (Gratton, 2011). This resonates with the implications of emergence – namely, that organisational change and practice are mediated through innumerable local interactions.

Research suggests that dispersed opportunities for initiative and boundary-crossing that promote connectivity between organisational members across the organisation (McElroy, 2010; Seel, 2006) are key organisational features favouring innovation and entrepreneurial practice. Opportunities for the widest range of stakeholders to generate innovations and participate in their development are important. Sometimes referred to as democratic or distributed innovation, this process involves firms and industries adapting in response to the pressures they face by dismantling traditional staff structures and divisions (Von Hippel, 2005). Another influential idea is that of co-production, a service-focused approach to innovation in public services which puts the service user rather than the policy maker or professional at the heart of this process (Osborne et al., 2013; Schlappa and Imani, 2012, forthcoming). It reflects a shift of focus from individualistic entrepreneurship to distributed agency (Miettinen, 2013).

As well as factors such as involving a wide spread of people and the crossing of traditional boundaries, the nature of the interaction is also found to be important. Research suggests that collaborative interaction is conducive to innovation: co-operation is better for innovation than reliance on top-down procedures. Reijo Miettinen, for example, highlights the importance of intertwining 'individual and collaborative agency' and suggests that 'interactive learning and interactions between key institutions are essential mechanisms of innovation' (Miettinen, 2013: 130, 42). Enabling ideas to cross the internal and external boundaries of organisations – open innovation – is seen as being of enormous value for the initiation and progress of innovation in industry (Chesborough, 2006). The attractions of open innovation go beyond private industry however. The paradigmatic shift in higher education and other areas is to 'systemic models of innovation ... [and] nonlinear dynamic, models of experimentation with open ends, a complex interplay of actors, an explosion of innovative ideas ... [and] a drift into many parallel ideas, actors, transactions and contexts' (Weber, 2013: 4). Indeed, in the public sector the term 'open innovation' can be fashioned more persuasively and more radically as 'social innovation'. The latter embraces the idea of citizens being involved in collective problem-solving through 'co-creating, co-designing and co-evaluating social goods and services', giving new impetus to ideas such co-creation and co-production which were introduced in the 1970s (Peters and Heraud, 2015: 8). Innovation benefits from the collaborative efforts to improve services between professionals and service users where it succeeds in enabling shared learning between the different stakeholders (Schlappa and Imani, 2012).

In a school context, an example of the intertwining of individual and collaborative agency referred to above can be found in the story of Melissa Oyediwura, a teacher who led a project to develop children's character through the implicit and explicit teaching of virtues (Oyediwura and Gaiteri, 2017). Melissa was supported in leading this project by participation in a Teacher Led Development Work group which took place at her school. The school's headteacher, Tracy, acted as a co-tutor of this group and encouraged all group members to think differently about leadership, to recognise their own capacity to lead the changes which resonated with their educational values.

Melissa's project focused on the development of children's character by the implicit and explicit teaching of virtues. The project arose out of Melissa's concern for children who struggled to regulate their emotions and hence their behaviour. Instead of the usual behaviour management strategies, Melissa took the innovative step of introducing character education, with the ultimate aim of supporting human flourishing. A colleague who heard Melissa talk about her project at a staff development event was inspired by its impact on children's attitudes and behaviours and asked Melissa if they could work collaboratively. This allowed the project to gain momentum across the school.

The impressive impact of this project, with children becoming 'ambassadors of a virtue' (Oyediwura and Gaiteri, 2017: 9), was secured at least to some degree through its collaborative nature. Melissa could have conducted her project in isolation within the school. Instead, as a result of sharing her project with her headteacher and other colleagues, the ways of working she developed are now a key part of a whole school approach to developing children in the broadest sense.

Research into teachers' knowledge development indicates the value of collaborative professional networks. Although more needs to be learnt about educational networks and the spread of innovation, it appears that social dynamics – 'the interplay between different stakeholders – policy-makers, researchers, teachers, students, parents, etc. – and between the elements of the social environment' – is a crucial dimension of enhancing knowledge and facilitating innovation (Révai and Guerriero, 2017: 66).

The implications of open or social innovation point to the need for leadership to emerge from diverse people and groupings across and beyond organisations. It suggests that staff and students are more likely to be innovative where leadership is distributed and there is a more open, democratic way of working. It underlines the importance of leadership distribution, which facilitates sharing and developing new ideas and knowledge, trying out new practices and learning from these and involving a range of people in developing and evaluating new practices.

Arguably, the valuing of open or social innovation promotes – or at least provides conditions which help to encourage – the tackling of inequalities in social justice. Collaboration and the involvement of people from different organisational levels and contexts (in the case of a school, students, teachers, support staff, senior leaders and so on) are integral to creating innovative cultures in all kinds of organisations. New ideas and practices are evaluated from differing perspectives and therefore have a better chance of being improved and working well. The influence of marketising and instrumentalising trends and of power differences means that open innovation is not necessarily more democratic or active in enhancing social justice. Hence it is necessary to explicitly incorporate into leadership aspirations to social justice and democratic values, which we encapsulate in the philosophy of co-development.

Democratic citizenship

A third challenge for schools is to promote democratic citizenship and an appreciation of values such as justice, democracy, the rule of law, tolerance, mutual understanding and a concern for the welfare of others. This can be seen as a challenge arising from policy frameworks in which schools in the UK and elsewhere are working. Many in the educational policy community, and others concerned with schooling, believe there is a need for school education to respond to global trends, such as the increased contacts and movements of people across national borders, consequent changes in national and local communities and the recognition that many problems facing the contemporary world cannot be addressed by nations acting separately. UNESCO (United Nations Educational, Scientific and Cultural Organisation) (2015: 14) has promoted global citizenship education since 2012, recognising that:

> An increasingly globalised world has raised questions about what constitutes meaningful citizenship as well as about its global dimensions. Although the notion of citizenship that goes beyond the nation state is not new, changes in the global context – for example, the establishment of international conventions and treaties, the growth of transnational organisations, corporations and civil society movements, and the development of international human rights frameworks – have significant implications for global citizenship.

Many national governments express concern about fostering democratic citizenship and the values essential to a free and tolerant society. Whilst the understandings of democracy and the historical contexts of countries vary, and the challenges faced or perceived in different nations differ between nations and over time, some consistent concern can be seen that sets a context for school education.

> In established democracies, such as those of Western Europe and North America, in newly established democratic states, such as those of Eastern and Central Europe and Latin America and, indeed, in countries taking steps towards democracy, there is a recognition that democracy is essentially fragile and that it depends on the active engagement of citizens, not just in voting, but in developing and participating in sustainable and cohesive communities. This, in turn, implies education for democratic citizenship. (Osler and Starkey, 2006: 434)

A concern with democratic citizenship is relevant to school education for reasons that are additional to – and arguably deeper than – the need to respond to requirements set by the policy context of a school. Developing as an individual in society with others – locally, nationally and globally – is an essential component of growing and learning as a person. So too is understanding the challenge of environmental change and pollution, and the alternative ways of living that are given practical expression in green schools (Kensler and Uline, 2017). In her analysis of the great global challenges, from climate crisis to education, Jennifer Gidley identifies the need for much enhanced development of capacities for creativity, imagination, critical thinking and complexity (Gidley, 2017: 131) and for seeing ourselves as 'the creative agents of our desired futures' (Gidley, 2016: 116).

What can the role of leadership distribution be in this, in particular where it takes the form of collaborative leadership? Leadership that is distributed and, crucially, that integrates the value-base we commend, reflecting a philosophy of co-development, enables experiential learning of equity and democratic values. The practice of such leadership, by those in non-positional roles such as students, as well as positional leaders, constitutes experience of living in a way that advances social justice and puts into practice the values of democratic citizenship. It can make practices such as collaboration, participation, discussion and learning from others' viewpoints part of the everyday life of the school for staff and students. The results of years of work sustained at the University of Cambridge in developing schools as democratic communities of learning and leadership were analysed with David Frost. The conclusion of this analysis was that creating such participative school environments enhances 'deep learning' – that is, learning that enhances self-awareness, critical thinking, autonomy and the process of becoming a person in the sense of 'developing the virtues, values and capacity for reason that enable us to live the "good life" and to take our places in the public sphere' (Frost and Roberts, 2011: 68). As Michael Fielding and Peter Moss (2011: 67) argue, progressive schooling and democracy as a way of living are about 'personal growth and transformation through achieved experience'.

Collaborative leadership by its nature is intended to encourage democratic citizenship through experiential learning about democracy and social justice. It allows students to experience in practice what democratic citizenship is like. Through this, students can learn what it means to respect in day-to-day life values such as justice, tolerance, mutual understanding and a concern for the welfare of others, and to ensure that no-one is excluded from opportunities to participate and learn. Integral to collaborative leadership is a concern for inclusion – who is able to speak and be heard, who is able to help shape change, who benefits; and who is marginalised in all these things. Collaborative learning, for example, is not truly collaborative if some are systematically less involved and less well placed to engage in learning than others. Fair opportunities for participation are integral to deliberative and holistic democracy. The practice of collaborative leadership helps to ensure challenging, critical questions are raised about fairness and who is privileged and who is left out, and how such issues might be tackled.

Factors conducive to leadership distribution working well

Creating a school culture in which leadership is distributed is not a once-and-for-all achievement but a practice that is likely to be advanced over time and to be developed in different ways and to varying degrees according to variable factors affecting local settings (Woods and Woods [G.J.], 2012). Leadership distribution and putting democratic and social justice values into practice are neither automatic nor easy. As is recognised in Chapter 3, leadership distribution does not necessarily generate beneficial effects: effects may be neutral or negative (Leithwood and Mascall, 2008; Louis et al., 2010: 21). Research suggests that distributed forms of leadership work better in certain conditions or where certain organisational features are well developed. Five factors conducive to leadership distribution being beneficial are highlighted in this section.

The first is a strong degree of co-ordination and planning of roles, expectations and modes of working together. Kenneth Leithwood et al. (2006: 61) refer to this as 'planful alignment'. The need for frameworks of support and clear, stated principles to support the flourishing of shared and teacher leadership is underlined in the Leadership for Learning project, referred to earlier in the chapter, and the HertsCam Network. The Leadership for Learning project was designed to explore leadership, learning and their interrelationship outside of the dominant performative educational discourse. Working with schools, the team offered a discursive approach to developing a set of intellectual and practical tools, designed to support both individual and organisational learning (Frost et al., 2008). The HertsCam Network is an independent teacher-led, not-for-profit organisation committed to educational transformation through support for teacher leadership.[3] In both of its core programmes, facilitators are supported by principles and guidance on processes to support teachers in effecting change through the initiation, design and leadership of development projects, including a collection of tools which they can draw from and develop (Hill, 2014).

The second factor is a cohesive culture. It is important for the organisational or group culture to have shared goals and values (Louis et al., 2010; Slavin, 2010; Woods [G.J.] and Woods, 2008) and a culture of trust (Kensler, 2008: cvi; Day et al., 2009: 189). The effectiveness of a culture of shared leadership is related to, *inter alia*, a sense of collective responsibility for student learning (Louis et al., 2010: 51). A review of co-operative learning concluded that 'most use of co-operative learning is informal, and does not incorporate the group goals and individual accountability that research has identified to be essential' (Slavin, 2010: 173). In a study of collegial leadership in a Steiner school, it was found that key aspects of the culture (shared philosophy, language and positive valuations

---

3 More information on the HertsCam Network can be found at www.hertscam.org.uk.

of freedom of interpretation and the importance of bringing spiritual awareness into everyday actions and decision-making) provided important substantive resources for staff to work with as co-leaders (Woods [G.J.] and Woods, 2008). Trust is found both to be an important mediating variable between democratic organisation and professional learning (Kensler, 2008: cvi) and 'a pre-requisite for the progressive and effective distribution of leadership' (Day et al., 2009: 189).

The first two factors – strong co–ordination and planning, and a cohesive culture – are indicative of the need for 'firm framing' which has been suggested to be an important feature of democratic leadership. That is, a clear framework of values, purpose and structures is a positive contributor to enabling the practice of democratic leadership. Part of this means developing a clear and considered value-base. For collaborative leadership, we commend consideration of the values of a philosophy of co-development for such a value-base.

The third factor is a focus on the organisation's core purpose, which for schools includes learning. A 'focus of distributed leadership on the core work of the organisation' creates 'strong links between leadership and learning' (Timperley and Robertson, 2011: 6).[4] Concerning another form of less hierarchical and more fluid relationships – learning communities – Louise Stoll (2011: 108) argues that their *raison d'être* depends on their being able to 'sharpen' their 'focus on improving or transforming mutually agreed-on areas of student learning'.

The fourth factor is capacity in terms of people's capabilities to engage in leadership practice. This refers both to an organisation's present capacity and its ability to nurture and grow that capacity over time. The major study by Day et al. (2009: 142), mentioned earlier in the chapter, suggested that 'there is a need to develop people before leadership can be effectively distributed' and explained,

> The promotion of leadership among a broad range of staff through training pro-grammes needs to take account of the readiness and abilities of staff to exercise responsibilities with accountabilities. Such readiness may take time and may not always be evident in the early phase of improvement. (Day et al., 2009: 4)

The importance of preparing students to undertake student leadership has been found to be of crucial importance in securing their success in this role (Frost and MacBeath, 2010). The demands of leadership distribution on senior leaders and their need for opportunities to develop their capacity for this are similarly significant factors to recognise and address. Alma Harris argues that distributed leadership requires a changed role for the principal or headteacher. She suggests that there are implications for what is expected of the senior leader, which include 'some relinquishment of power and authority which will be difficult for

---

4   See also Robinson (2006) and Robinson et al. (2008).

some principals' and 'a high degree of trust to negotiate successfully the fault lines of formal and informal leadership practice' (Harris, 2012: 15–16). Training for headteachers needs 'to encompass greater attention to the process of distributing leadership and the practicalities of ensuring effective patterns of distribution' (Day et al., 2009: 4).

We would caution against adopting a simple linear model of preparing or training teachers and others first and then implementing leadership distribution. The fostering of leadership capabilities is an ongoing process that includes both support and activity (experiential learning) by teachers and others. The Teacher Led Development Work programme of the HertsCam Network, for example, involves both guided sessions for teachers led by facilitators and the practice of teacher-led change by those teachers who write up accounts and evidence which are shared with colleague teachers as a way of collectively developing their learning of what is involved in teacher leadership (Woods et al., 2016). A learning model of leadership development that conceptualises this kind of approach is discussed in Chapter 7.

The fifth factor is effective internal accountability. Internal accountability needs to be considered in order to avoid the situation in which everyone is accountable with the result that no-one is actually accountable. Just as effective collaborative learning is also found to require individual accountability (Slavin, 2010), so leadership distribution needs a strong internal accountability system (Day et al., 2009: 117). In other words, accountability has to be felt individually as well as being shared.

This is not necessarily just about upward accountability – that is, accountability through a hierarchical structure of formal authority. There are different forms of accountability. There is professional accountability to obligations, values and codes of practice that are incumbent on practitioners in a profession; there are also commitments to wider cultural values, such as to truth, the pursuit of knowledge and justice.[5] Senior leaders can be accountable to staff and students too, through for example 'soft accountability' strategies that may include transparency about decisions and open access to reviews of senior leaders' performance (Sorensen, 2010: 9; Woods, 2011: 161).

Summary

This chapter has set out some of the reasons that leadership distribution is important and the benefits that can arise through it, considered under the headings of learning, innovation and democratic citizenship. The chapter acknowledged the

---

5 See, for example, Scott (1989) whose typology of responsiveness is discussed in Woods et al. (1998: 147–148).

challenges in generating evidence of such benefits. These include the difficulty of defining in measurable terms leadership distribution, which is inevitably a diffuse practice with different elements to it, and the complexity of influences and variables in which leadership distribution takes place, which makes it problematic to assign a simple cause-and-effect relationship between leadership distribution and outcomes. The nature, context and development of leadership distribution are by no means uniform. This means that important choices have to be made in developing and sustaining leadership distribution – about the purpose and practice of leadership distribution and about how it should be supported and nurtured.

Despite definitional problems, research on leadership distribution has a common concern with leadership approaches that share an intention to enable school members in non-positional roles to take initiatives and to enact and collaborate in change. The findings of such studies have, we would argue, a shared orientation to leadership practices that differ significantly from traditional top-down leadership. The range of studies and the use of both quantitative and qualitative methods to explore leadership distribution and its effects help considerably in gaining some idea of the influences such leadership can have.

The accumulating findings of these studies are, therefore, instructive. The chapter acknowledged that there are studies that have not found a positive relationship between leadership distribution and learning. Nevertheless, we concluded that there is a range of studies suggesting evidence of some positive relationship between leadership distribution and learning, innovation and democratic citizenship. In addition, it was emphasised that any benefits of leadership distribution do not occur automatically. Research suggests a number of factors that are important in helping to ensure that leadership distribution has beneficial impacts. These include strong co-ordination and planning, a cohesive culture that involves shared goals and values, a clear focus on the organisation's core purpose, development of people's capabilities to share in leadership, and effective internal accountability so that each individual feels a responsibility to the collaborative work.

In relation specifically to the collaborative leadership we are setting out in this book, our proposition is that the required cohesive culture, of a group or school, benefits from an explicit consideration and integration of the values of a philosophy of co-development.

In the next chapter we turn to critiques and challenges concerning leadership distribution. Appreciating these is vital in developing a robust conception of collaborative leadership that understands both the distributed character of leadership and the necessity to attend critically to its values and purpose.

3

CRITIQUES AND CHALLENGES

Introduction

This chapter engages with some of the key, critical concerns about leadership distribution, in relation both to the concept of distributed leadership and more widely leadership distribution as a practice, however that is named, and its policy context. What might be seen otherwise as a neat trajectory – from the dependence spawned by hierarchy to the freedom of leadership distribution – is problematised by highlighting important critiques and challenges. We turn first to critiques concerning the conceptualisation of distributed leadership, and then to critiques of leadership distribution around issues of educational purpose, social justice, power and inequalities. Three challenges are then highlighted in turn: the persistence of the 'heroic' leader model, uncertainties that can arise with freedom, and feasibility. Understanding this range and nature of critiques and challenges is important before moving onto explaining our conception of collaborative leadership in Chapters 4 and 5.

Conceptualising distributed leadership

The challenge of conceptualising distributed leadership was identified by a seminal review of the literature published in 2003 which concluded that there were 'few clear definitions' (Bennett et al., 2003: 6). A more recent meta-analysis took the view that defining such leadership remained a problem, with no 'universally accepted definition of distributed leadership' being apparent (Tian et al., 2016: 156). Alma Harris and John DeFlaminis (2016), however, are less convinced that no progress has been made. Instead they remind us of the many valuable examples of the practical application of distributed leadership contained in the wealth of research conducted in recent years. Other writers go further, questioning the wisdom of the search for definitions and arguing that 'providing a definitive definition would inevitably fail to capture the complexity, and inherent paradoxes of the field and would potentially foreclose a series of ongoing debates and discussions' (Bolden, 2011: 256).

Our view is that advances have been made in awareness of the different ways in which distributed leadership can be conceptualised and in asking critical questions about what this means for our understanding of it. However, it remains essential to formulate explicitly and critically how one conceptualises distributed leadership for the specific purpose at hand – which may be for practical change, for research purposes or a combination of change and enquiry. Different definitions may be intended to do different things. For example, some conceptualisations are intended to be *descriptive*. These claim to portray what leadership is. The work by Cecil Gibb (1968), for example, led to his claim that, if you observe leadership, it actually *is* the outcome of a process that passes between people: this is the way things are.[1] Other conceptualisations assert that introducing or increasing distributed leadership amongst a group or organisation will lead to improved outcomes. The implication of this view is that policy-makers and senior leaders ought to promote distributed leadership. This is an *evaluative* kind of definition, as it carries an imperative that leadership distribution *ought* to be done.[2]

An evaluative definition that is framed in terms of improved organisational outcomes, especially outcomes such as grades and attainment scores in a school, suggests an instrumental logic is being used: the overriding benefit is a functional

---

1 For an animated exposition of this view, see 'Leadership is … Distributed', a videoscribe created by P.A. Woods and A. Roberts at www.youtube.com/watch?v=J5F0MNrDSpY, published 22 September 2013.

2 In relation to Gibb, see Gibb (1968) as well as Gronn (2002) and Woods and Woods [G.J.] (2013). Normative or evaluative conceptualisations are discussed in Woods (2015a).

one of achieving measurable organisational goals. Another kind of evaluative conceptualisation may be based on intrinsic values that are claimed to be associated with distributed leadership. Distributed leadership from this viewpoint is intrinsically desirable because there are, it is claimed, inherent benefits – such as greater respect, freedom or virtue – when working in a distributed leadership culture.

Our work in a European network of policy-makers, practitioners and scholars led to the formulation of a conception of distributed leadership for equity and learning – a conceptualisation of leadership that integrates both an evaluative dimension based on certain values and a descriptive dimension by acknowledging that leadership has a distributed character (Woods, 2015a; Woods and Roberts, 2015). We have built upon the understanding which came from this and other projects in developing the view of leadership set out in this book which encompasses a value-base, expressed as a philosophy of co-development, and a descriptive recognition of leadership as being characterised by intentionality and emergence.

Critiquing leadership distribution

The second, and much more significant concern, is the argument that the practice and investigation of distributed leadership, and of moves generally towards leadership distribution, often avoid critical issues of profound importance. These include matters of social justice, power and inequalities, as well as how distributed leadership is influenced by the educational policies that shape the aims of education. An approach that digs deeper into leadership distribution, to face such matters, needs to ask three questions (Woods and Woods [G.J.], 2013):

- What is it being used for (purpose)?
- What assumptions are being made about personal development and learning (the self)?
- What are its implications for social justice and inequalities (power)?

A prominent critique in relation to the first question is that leadership distribution has been harnessed to marketising and performative agendas that narrow educational purpose. Attempts to extend leadership distribution face the challenging question of the extent to which they are in practice serving economistic and performative aims. Leadership distribution can thus be seen as another way of controlling the identities and practice of those who work in schools. Critical research suggests that the apparent freedoms of open innovation (Chapter 2) mask their real effects in forging professional identities committed to the policy requirements of the centre and the functional, narrowing values and goals of performative governance dominated by instrumental rationality.

In a study of middle leaders, Linda Hammersley-Fletcher and Michael Strain (2011: 881) conclude that distributed leadership, enacted through labelling of staff as leaders, diverts attention from the key purpose of learning:

> The evidence ... would seem to suggest that successful middle leaders become efficient at creating new bases of evidence to demonstrate compliance and recognition in respect of implementing government policies and the head's agendas, rather than using their role to develop significant initiatives in learning and teaching practices. Thus it seems right to question the relevance and validity of current notions of multi-layered leadership. The notion that teachers need to be labelled 'leader' in order to be pro-active in their role is also open to question.

David Hall et al. (2013: 484–485), in a study of five case study schools, conclude that, whilst the 'influence of DL was found to be strong with a wide range of different individuals and groups in the school eager to discursively associate themselves with this term',

> the need to comply with and act in accordance with nationally ordained policies remained pressing. In this tightly controlled environment opportunities to exert agency outside of this regime were found to be strictly limited ... on the one hand a discursive intervention that those working within schools, not least designated senior leaders, found very difficult to resist, on the other the requirement to perform according to a pre-determined and closely controlled set of requirements.

In one of Hall et al.'s case study schools, recognition of the dominance of the headteacher's view of leadership, including how he conceived of distributed leadership, was widely shared, as was the pressure to increase attainment and performance as determined by national criteria, so as to do well in Ofsted (Office for Standards in Education) inspections. Staff largely supported the headteacher's strong espousal of distributed leadership, though they were found to interpret it in different ways. The headteacher described distributed leadership in ways that likened it to delegation – handing work down to subordinates – and saw it as working in parallel with his being, as he put it, a 'charismatic hero' kind of leader (Hall et al., 2013: 481). A senior leader explained that 'the remit I've been given from [the headteacher] is that the next Ofsted we have outstanding at teaching and learning, so basically my job description is to get us there' (quoted in Hall et al., 2013: 480). Staff were strongly supportive of the view that distributed leadership was being enacted in the school, that they are afforded autonomy in their work and that, whilst there remains a strong hierarchy, they could also exercise leadership at different levels of the school. Some were unsure as to how to define or describe distributed leadership. One 'emerging leader' in the school expressed the view that distributed leadership is a way of getting access to information and insights that help 'lower' staff gain promotion

(Hall et al., 2013: 482). For Hall et al., the general support given to the view that leadership is distributed is explained by the dominance of the headteacher in this school, more than by a fundamental change in leadership practice.

> Given [the headteacher's] dominant position in the authority structure of the school and the use of the term 'DL' by senior members of staff and [the headteacher] himself, it can be viewed as hardly surprising that such discursive affirmation is replicated amongst those lower down in the hierarchy. In order to 'get on' or survive in this organisation it is necessary to be seen as supporting the Principal and other powerful members of the leadership team and potentially dangerous, in career terms at least, to be challenging ideas publicly discussed in an approving and approved manner. This process of not challenging the Principal and affirming top down discursive edicts can be viewed as central to the logic of this institution. (Hall et al., 2013: 483)

The practice of distributed leadership 'suggests a discursive softening of the harsher edges of managerialism', though 'in an environment where institutional and personal attachments to those instrumentalist and performative agendas so central to NPM [New Public Management] remain strong' (Hall et al., 2013: 485). Critical research suggests that, as in this example, the apparent freedoms of leadership dispersed across more open and fluid organisational boundaries mask their real effects. In practice, these effects are the forging of professional identities committed to the policy requirements of the centre and to an instrumental rationality – that is, professional practice in which priority is given to devising the means of achieving measurable ends defined by the narrowing values and goals of performative governance. (See, for example, Ball, 2006; Jeffrey and Troman, 2012a/b; Martin and Learmouth, 2012; Scott, 2010).

From data gathered during an ethnographic study of six primary schools in England, Bob Jeffrey and Geoff Troman seek to show how a policy context driven by performative and competitive principles shapes the schools' institutional environments and leads to changes in professional commitments and identities. They argue from their data that the latter come to be focused more on institutional developments and needs than on broader professional values. Jeffrey and Troman (2012a: 197) refer to the kind of school formed in this context as 'the embracing performative institution' (EPI). The EPI school shapes the identity of teachers and other school members through, *inter alia*, the ways in which they are 'embraced' by team work, nurturing and distributed leadership. Jeffrey and Troman (2012a: 203) paint a picture in their reporting of the study of how they see these types of schools from the data they gathered:

> The embracing institution is constituted by a 'negotiated order' (Strauss, 1978) ... The EPI contains more flattened hierarchies, where members develop the institution. ... Today's professional primary school teacher is a team player in open competition with other school teams, but also part of a team that needs to present itself as a unified, creative, inclusive and effective managerial organisation ...

The study found that professional cohesion and good professional relations were essential to the development of the team approach. More than this, the study concludes that these are 'corporate teams' that 'reflect the modern commercial organisation in which everyone plays a part in the development and promotion of the cultural institution'. The following is a cited example of the researchers' observations (Jeffrey and Troman, 2012a: 203):

> I find, in the staffroom, a display board entitled 'Staff Achievement Board', with some displayed certificates on which some members of staff have been commended for certain actions or for just starting a new role. All staff are encouraged to download a copy and to fill it in for someone they think worthy. The TEAM approach 'Together Everyone Achieves More' is written in large letters above the main notice board and outside at least one classroom. (FN, C, 26 February 2007)

The researchers suggest that the 'most significant aspect of these embracing institutions was the care they exhibited towards members, bringing them close to the institution's cultural life and development'; quoting one of the teachers (Jeffrey and Troman, 2012a: 203):

> We do a lot of professional development. We have specialists in to motivate us and I think that really does keep you going. We try to nurture each other and help each other and we're all very hot on family links and we do that with the class but we also try to do that with each other and support each other and have networks and have teams.

The crucial role of the headteacher is emphasised, as in the case study schools researched by Hall and colleagues cited above. Jeffrey and Troman (2012a: 204) quote a headteacher:

> I don't do many of the things I should do as a Head, I don't take many assemblies, I never cover classes, I don't do very much paper work. I've got brilliant people in the office and brilliant people in the leadership team. I don't do that, what I do is influence. I influence children; I influence parents and carers.

The argument developed by Jeffrey and Troman is that staff feel there is much that is positive in these schools, but that there are also practices and a dominant language that results in school members being socialised into a culture of business and discourse more than a culture of public professionalism. As one teacher explains, they have 'ownership of the school and its policies and its beliefs … it's engrained in staff as soon as you come in' (Jeffrey and Troman, 2012a: 204). From one viewpoint, it may be considered that there is much to be commended in the distributed approach to leadership in such schools. For critical studies, however, it is not opportunities for creative professional leadership that are distributed through greater autonomy for professionals and others in schools. Rather, it is a commitment to the more competitive and business-like environment that measures education through exams and tests that purport to show learning attainment against standardised models of progress.

Hence, the argument from critical research is that any autonomy created is shaped and distorted by the objective conditions created by policy – specifically the powers and expectations of a governance system driven by performative and competitive principles. A subjective sense of professional identity is created that ensures *compliance* to these principles. Such compliance does not mean that the school environments are experienced entirely or even mostly in negative terms by school staff and students. Mutual support and caring for colleagues can be a part of the daily practice that is valued by school members. The positive experiencing of change – as well as negative experiences of domination and work intensification (Gronn, 2003) – reinforces the complexity of organisations and everyday practices that complexity theory highlights.

As researchers, we have to be alert to the challenge that theory – such as the proposition that performative identities are being fostered – can override or obscure aspects of the expressed experience of school members. Teachers and others may experience professional and educational benefits resulting from the kind of autonomy they consider they have. It is important to consider the extent to which this challenges or even undermines critical theorisation that foregrounds negative connotations of discourses that claim organisational changes are enhancing autonomy and leadership distribution.

The value of critical research, nevertheless, is that it helps to surface an understanding of underlying aspects of the environment developing in many schools which are damaging to genuine autonomy, professional agency and the deep learning discussed below. Leadership distribution, from this critical perspective, is enmeshed in the culture of performative governance that affects public services. In these services, policy and organisational climates are dominated by an instrumental rationality which promotes an entrepreneurial culture, with progress and achievement measured relentlessly against calculable ends such as targets and financial goals (Ward et al., 2015; Woods, 2011, 2013). Individuals and organisations are encouraged to 'become committed to improvement in outputs measured against competing peers and institutions, a defining characteristic of markets and one which encourages continual improvement to maintain market position' (Jeffrey and Troman, 2012b: 485). In such a climate, leadership distribution is too often harnessed to meet educational policy goals which push schooling 'towards standardized practices and outcomes which can be audited easily' (Hartley, 2009: 282).

The second question to deepen our understanding of leadership distribution is about the self. What conception of the self underpins leadership distribution and the learning which it is intended to foster? To what extent is leadership distribution implicated in promoting learning that is confined by a constricted view of what it means to grow and flourish as a person? This is closely related to and overlaps with the first issue of purpose. The specific challenge is the extent to which performative and standardised models of educational attainment drive the focus of leadership distribution.

To the extent that leadership distribution is assimilated into marketising and performative policy agendas, it is deployed to support a narrow view of learning and personal development. This kind of narrow learning is focused on 'high-stakes testing which leads us down a blind alley where the superficial rehearsal of second-hand, off-the peg knowledge which helps our students to pass exams is mistaken for actual learning' (Frost and Roberts, 2011: 67). The ethnographic study of primary schools cited above found school cultures 'imbued with awards and rewards' for breaking through 'learning barriers' and 'for producing performances' for each other and others (such as parents and the community), 'as well as against each other internally in the shape of sports and other competitions and against other schools' (Jeffrey and Troman, 2014: 74). As noted above, the experience could be positive – people 'including learners played the game with apparent joy and the raising of self-esteem and gained satisfaction from the process of performance outcomes' (Jeffrey and Troman, 2012b: 485). The study provides evidence of how learning is seen by some school students and how they are engaged in constructing and conveying a way of understanding their learning.

In this extract from the data (Jeffrey and Troman, 2014: 75) the researcher (R) is exploring children's perceptions of Standard Assessment Tests (SATs), taken in primary schools in England when a child is aged 6–7 and 10–11.

> Jo: The SATs are a test of what the teachers have been teaching us and how good our teachers are teaching us. If the teacher doesn't teach you hardly anything or if you don't understand quite as much because it hasn't been explained you'll get another level.
>
> R: But who tests the teacher?
>
> Jo: The government.
>
> R: How do you know that?
>
> Jo: Because my mother told me that the teachers get tested that's why we do SATs.
>
> G: Our teacher told us that our SATs go to the government and if we mess it up the government won't be happy with our work, that's what Miss E. said.
>
> R: Does that worry you?
>
> G: Yes, in case our work's rubbish and if I only got 4 questions right out of 20 I don't think the government would be happy with us. (City – Year 5)

Here, pupils clearly understand SATs as high stakes testing – both children and their teachers are judged by them and risk censure if they do not demonstrate progress. This potential censure extends to the school itself, affecting its place amongst other schools and eventually its survival (Jeffrey and Troman, 2014: 75).

R: Why are people making you do these SATs?

Ma: To see where you are.

R: But you know where you are, you've been told.

Ma: Making sure for secondary school, maybe.

C: So our school can show the secondary school and they can place you in a higher group or a lower group. It would be good for them if we got higher results, City school would have a good name for itself among other schools.

Ma: You don't want other people thinking our school is no good because people are getting low SATs results, kids won't come to this school. (City – Year 6)

The delicacy or vulnerability of human-ness is important to consider in relation to the self and learning. In some ways people are, as living things often tend to be, strong and resilient. People can survive, even grow, in difficult conditions that test them. However, people can also be deeply affected for the worse by the contexts in which they find themselves. Learning is a process sensitive to its environment. The metaphor of the picture frame, suggested by the sociologist Simmel, is helpful in recognising this (see Simmel, 1997: 141; Woods, 2005: 88). The frame provides the support and protection for the fragile and important part of the painting – the picture itself. If we think of learning and human growth as the fragile part of education, the outer 'firm framing' is provided by institutional structures and cultures around the human process of learning. From a critical perspective, a performative and instrumentally driven approach reduces the painting, the learning and human growth, to painting by numbers: How many numbered spaces have been painted in? Was the right colour used, as directed by the central designer? The 'quality' of painting can be calculated by simple measures in response to these questions. However, the fullness and diversity, the sense of self which a painting may express, is lost.

Leadership distribution by its nature does not have to be committed to a narrowing, test-focused agenda. In terms of the metaphor of the picture frame, it is not committed to framing paintings that consist of painting by numbers. Leadership distribution may give priority to educational aims based in a more expansive view of the person, leading to a holistic perspective of human development and a concern to foster 'deep learning'. By deep learning we are referring to

the development of understanding and personal meaning which have a transformative effect on learners. Deep learning is empowering because it leads not only to enhanced capability in life but also to greater self-awareness, critical thinking and autonomy ... [and involves] developing the virtues, values and capacity for reason that enable us to live the 'good life' and to take our places in the public sphere. (Frost and Roberts, 2011: 68)

A more holistic perspective on learning is integral to our view of collaborative leadership and the philosophy of co-development (see Chapter 5).

Concerning power – the third question – it is argued that, far from being more equal and democratic, leadership distribution can generate or widen power disparities. Attempts to distribute leadership do not necessarily shift power relationships and social injustices. Although leadership distribution may appear to promise more fair, even democratic, leadership practice this is not necessarily the case. Jacky Lumby concludes from her analysis of power and distributed leadership, that the 'central issue of power surfaces only superficially, if at all, in much of the literature': she goes on to argue that, however, we should not underestimate the power of distributed leadership to 'enact inequality' through the unthinking acceptance – as leadership is distributed – of prevailing assumptions, established power differences and the 'banal' everyday marginalisation of certain voices (Lumby, 2013: 583, 592).

Studies show that micro-politics can exert a malign influence on relationships. Factors – such as gender, force of personality, assumptions about less experienced teachers – can lead to some being unfairly marginalised (Woods, 2016b). (We discuss in Chapter 6 different kinds of authority that may be given or withheld in the process of leadership distribution.) Some are positioned less well than others to participate and exercise influence in organisations where efforts are made to distribute leadership. A study of teachers' perceptions in China found that although forms of distributed leadership may be implemented, the way it is operationalised can retain a dominative hierarchy and wide power distances. Distributed leadership was most frequently manifested in the top–down pyramid structure with a high-power distance: the results of the study showed that the higher the position one had in the hierarchy, the more resources one possessed and the more agency one practised (Tian, 2016). Only a fifth of teachers reported experiencing the kind of leadership distribution which accords with the flexible, emergent and practice-centred distributed leadership model (Tian, 2016). In a case study of teacher leadership in a US school, it was found that male teachers were accorded greater legitimacy as influencers and non-positional power holders through the greater professional cultural authorisation that others ascribed to them in relation to school discipline and control (Scribner and Bradley-Levine, 2010; see also Woods, 2016b).

Research we have undertaken led us to identify two factors influential in creating such inequalities (Woods and Roberts, 2016). One is social positioning. By this we mean the process by which a person places individuals in relation to other school members, using as resources both their own interpretation and the existing social structures and ideas. For example, a school's formal hierarchy of authority positions individuals, but people also apply their own judgements of who is to be most respected as an authority. In this sense, authorisation is a process not a simple product of organisational, professional or social structures of relative respect. Other examples from our research involve perceptions of significant organisation and social boundaries. Some participants invited to share their experience of distributed leadership placed students outside the main, adult-defined school organisation, or explained how younger students were ascribed lower status as compared with the higher status of older students. We made the point that these placings or positionings should not be viewed as static 'givens', but rather as 'patterns that emerge and are reinforced (or challenged) through continuous processes in which people interact, create and interpret the organisation's stated aims and discourses about leadership and education' (Woods and Roberts, 2016: 152).

Another factor is the differential and unequal distribution of capitals (Woods and Roberts, 2016: 152). Capitals are properties of people and groups which influence their perceived relative worth, the social positioning just discussed and the exercise of influence and power. They include social capital (such as networks within the school) and professional capital, such as the possession of qualifications seen as relevant to professional practice (Noordegraaf and Schinkel, 2011). Examples affecting participation in distributed leadership included variations in social capital in terms of links and interactions with senior leaders; more of this kind of social capital in the school we studied was seen as advantageous in accessing resources and influencing decision-making. The more limited professional capital of support staff was seen as significant in giving them a more marginal position in relation to leadership in the school.

Dependence on senior leadership figures does not necessarily disappear with distributed leadership practices then, despite the intention to share opportunities for leadership initiative. Distributed leadership that is focused strongly 'on priorities from the school's improvement plan or the headteacher's priorities' can limit 'the scope for spontaneous leadership or for a grass roots change agenda' with teachers 'still waiting for permission to act' (Torrance, 2013: 57). Research in Finnish and Shanghai schools found that teachers wanted to be more engaged, 'not merely as resources but also as active agents', but the organisational perspective 'often prevailed over the individual perspective' (Tian, 2016: 53). This situation is illustrated in the following vignette which reflects on the development of a new school in China.

A new school, with a high level of autonomy, was to be established in a suburban area of Shanghai. The Principal and Vice-Principal came from an existing high-performing school. They wished to develop a new school in which teachers worked collaboratively with colleagues and the leadership team to move the school forward.

Together they appointed all the teachers for the new school. Their recruitment criteria required that each teacher had graduated from one of the top universities in China. This was seen as an indicator that the teacher would have been supported in developing critical thinking and skills in learning to learn. The Principal and Vice-Principal sought to recruit teachers with no previous leadership experience and whom they felt would be less likely to have a fixed authoritarian mindset.

There was some evidence of the practice of distributed leadership within the school, with numerous teachers being involved in leading different aspects of the school's work. However, much of the decision-making power remained with those in a traditional hierarchical position.

The role of the school Vice-Principal was critical because she was the ultimate responsibility bearer of all the school activities. The teachers counted on her to bring clarity and direction to their leadership work and ultimately to take over an activity herself if teachers failed to deliver what was needed for the organisation.

(The vignette is based on Tian, 2016 and e-mail correspondence with the researcher, Meng Tian.)

Persistence of the 'heroic' leader model

The development of leadership distribution that promotes connectivity and inter-dependence, rather than dependence and compliance, is engaged in shifting many of the existing assumptions about leadership. Western (2013: 274) describes the new, developing discourse as eco-leadership, which we discuss in Chapter 5, but observes guardedly that eco-leadership is 'growing but uncertainly'. After years of promoting ideas such as distributed leadership by many influential advocates and agencies, there is a long way to go in embedding this in schools. A major study of leadership in schools in England, for example, concluded that 'most schools continue to retain a traditional structure of a single headteacher and a wider leadership team', and found that aspects of 'hero' leadership continued in distributed forms of leadership (Earley et al., 2012: 111). A survey of teachers and school leaders across several European countries found a significant gap between school leaders' and teachers' perceptions. Although not a random sample, with consequent limits to the generalisability of its findings (Duif et al., 2013: 20–21), the gap is worth noting: 87% of school leaders perceived their practice as distributive compared with 39% of teachers (Duif et al., 2013: 34, 43). The same survey found marked differences between countries. Survey respondents in England and Scotland were much more likely to report distributive leadership practice than Italy and France (Duif et al., 2013: 34–35).

What accounts for the persistence of traditional hierarchical leadership and the 'heroic', top-down assumption of leadership? Firstly, there is the allure of the 'great leader'.

> The allure of leadership (or more importantly, of leaders) seems to retain its pull ...,
> as evidenced by our collective willingness to put hope into new political, commu-
> nity or business leaders while demonising others. The varieties change; from
> transformational to servant, from charismatic to quiet, but the concept itself seems
> to command our attention. (Ladkin, 2010: viii)

Secondly, there are interests that reinforce and maintain the momentum of the discourses that affirm the 'great leader' idea. An industry of books on leadership, for example, help to sustain this idea and promise ways by which aspirant leaders can attain the top spot. Working within a bureaucratic, hierarchical system reinforces the value of superiors in the system: a school's peer appraisal system found difficulties in maintaining confidence as some preferred returning to 'a hierarchical system where they could show their progress to someone who "mattered"' (Jones, 2015: 82). Thirdly, it is easy to revert to a linear input-process-output model. Agnieszka Bates (2016: 39) criticises Michael Fullan, noting that he 'ventures into the paradigm of complexity' but also 'tends to finish his argument with "lessons" that reduce complexity into prescriptions'. A fundamental misunderstanding that emergence can be 'designed', and hence controlled, persists in much mainstream management literature (Bates, 2016: 35; Stacey, 2010). The temptation is for senior managers to look for the techniques that will allow them to control complexity (Stacey, 2012).

The notion of framing helps us to understand the persistence of top-down, hierarchical leadership perspectives. People carry round familiar frames of meaning. An embedded, familiar frame provides an order of ideas, feelings and memories that guides responses to everyday experiences. It provides a set of markers, viewing points and associations that help the person interpret what they experience in organisational life. Joep Cornelissen and Mirjam Werner (2014: 214), in their review of work on framing, suggest that the notion of frames brings together the macro and micro levels of organisational life. They are 'virtual structures of meaning, present in day-to-day interactions, but not separate from ... local contexts'. The familiarity of traditional, top-down frames of leadership is in tension with the critical intentionality (Chapter 5) and the enabling structures, creative spaces and pro-active, boundary-spanning non-positional agency that we discuss in later chapters. The process of reframing leadership is highlighted in Chapter 10.

The uncertainty of freedom

A mirror image of concerns with control and power is the challenge of freedom and uncertainty. Acknowledging this uncertainty or risk is of particular importance to us given that a central aim of collaborative leadership as we view it is the nurturing of relational freedom.

In so far as leadership distribution facilitates more dispersed initiative – in other words, disperses power and authority – the question of how that freedom may be used is raised. And whilst it may be and is used for good educational purposes, individuals and groups may also use it with other aims in mind, such as protection of individual interests. This is part of the uncertainty appreciated by complexity theory. Leadership distribution involves the acceptance of a lack of control promised, if not delivered, by traditional hierarchical leadership. There is an observation, in a TV series *Only Fools and Horses*, made by a sailor who fought in the Second World War, to young people in peacetime: we fought to give you freedom and what do you do with it – anything you like!

Now leadership distribution may not lead to non-positional leaders doing anything they like, but if it frees people to make choices and decisions there is some risk. This is a thought-provoking reflection by David Frost (2011: 49) on one of the challenges concerning teacher led development projects:

> ... teachers who respond to the invitation to initiate and lead development work tend to be influenced by values of collaboration, openness, inclusivity, equity and other values which resonate with statements from the EU, UNICEF [United Nations Children's Fund], OSF [Open Society Foundation] and other bodies which would claim to be committed to social justice and democratisation. However, there may be a fear that, once teachers have more freedom to set the agenda, some might be influenced by more negative value positions such as extreme nationalism or religious intolerance.

Agreement about what constitutes the value-base and moral purpose of leadership practice cannot be assumed to be shared. In a later chapter we identify values-clarification as one of the key steps in leadership development. We also note there that imposing acceptance of a particular value-base, such as the philosophy of co-development that we commend in this book, would be counter to the spirit of this very same philosophy. Values, such as those of holistic democracy and relational freedom, need to grow and be nurtured through self-activity, dialogue and experiential learning (see Chapter 6). Part of that experience is taking a founding step of critically examining and elucidating one's own values, which we explain further in Chapter 10.

Feasibility

The final challenge we highlight is that of feasibility. One set of arguments against leadership distribution and democratisation concerns its practicality (Woods, 2011: 69–70). This includes a concern that there may be a lack of *democratic capacity*. It may be feared that if collaborative leadership practice were to be followed, there would an absence of the capabilities and skills that participants need to make leadership distribution, participation and collaborative activity work. The importance of people's capacity was highlighted amongst the factors conducive to leadership distribution working well in Chapter 2. There it was also observed that any leadership capacity needs to be viewed not as a problem to be fixed by a 'shot' of leadership development; the fostering of leadership capabilities, rather, is an ongoing process that includes both support and activity (experiential learning) by teachers and others.

A second practical critique is that of *inefficiency*. The concern from this viewpoint is that the time and effort given to advancing leadership distribution and invested by people across the organisation in doing leadership will detract from the organisation's effectiveness. Resources are tied up in widening leadership activity and in making collaborative processes work. The resources involved include time, any financial support for professional development or other supportive opportunities, and the intellectual and emotional labour that people put into leadership distribution. Collaborative leadership activity may, according to the topic, involve students, support staff, parents and/or teachers co-leading change. Working together as needed to clarify values, lead enquiry and research and develop innovations may be seen as slower than implementing 'good practice' gleaned from other schools and less directly beneficial than improving teaching through observation, appraisal and point-by-point improvement goals in order to demonstrate 'outstanding' teaching to inspectors. As is evident from the benefits of leadership distribution in Chapter 2, however, the potential for worthwhile outcomes and experience for everyone in the school – in quality of learning, successful innovation and gaining awareness about democratic citizenship through doing – is substantial.

A different kind of challenge is the *clash of logics* in modern organisations to which Woods and Gronn (2009) drew attention in their discussion of democratic organisation. From this viewpoint, democracy is seen as unsuited to organisations. As a way of governing society and political entities – local and national – it is entirely appropriate. The logic of discussion, debate, participation and collective decision-making are legitimate ways of enabling such entities to work.

For modern organisations, based on contracts between employer and staff, giving management the right to direct employees, the collaborative or democratic logic does not fit. The imperative is for staff to follow the instructions of management: the contractual relationship is one in which, in the sphere of working for that organisation, the employee is the dependent party (so long as the employer meets other agreed elements of the contract, such as pay, and legal requirements). Within a contractual logic, variations in leadership, such as distributed or shared leadership, are different, more subtle ways by which management exerts control, rather than representing the introduction of an alternative and challenging logic of organising working relationships.

Concern about the unsuitedness of a logic of practice that introduces participative and democratic values is challengeable, however. For example, not every aspect of working life, especially in services like education, can be reduced to contractual exchange. Teachers and other staff have principles and codes (professional and cultural) and moral commitments to what they are doing which they bring to their work and which introduce imperatives not necessarily covered by a contract. They also have rights that inhere in them as people to be respected and to be listened to. Then, additionally, there are parties to educational activity who are not covered by work contracts. Students, parents and local communities all have rights, responsibilities, interests and legitimate views on education as a process of growing as a human being. Recognising this allows for – indeed demands – the introduction of a logic other than contractualism.

Summary

This chapter has highlighted challenges and critiques concerning leadership distribution. The first raised was the conceptualisation of distributed leadership. We took the view that this was not a fundamental problem. Advances have been made in awareness of the different ways in which distributed leadership can be conceptualised and in asking critical questions about what this means for our understanding of it. What is essential is as much clarity as possible on how distributed leadership is being conceptualised for the specific purpose at hand, whether that be for research, practice improvement or a mixture of both.

A good deal of attention was given to discussing the second area of attention – critiques from critical research. In doing this, the chapter recognised the importance of tackling issues of purpose, self and power. Three critical questions were posed about leadership distribution concerning the extent to which it serves economistic and performative aims, promotes learning confined by a constricted view of what it means to grow and flourish as a person and fails to address unjust power differences and relational inequalities that condition effective involvement in leadership. These questions surface issues of acute importance that need to be faced wherever leadership distribution is developed and enhanced.

The challenge of the persistence of the 'heroic' leader model was considered and recognised as a deep-seated issue. We indicated that active reframing of views about leadership is an important response to this and a crucial part of developing collaborative leadership. A further challenge highlighted was uncertainty and the challenge of freedom. As leadership distribution facilitates more dispersed initiative and disperses power, the question of how that freedom may be used is raised. Whilst it may be and is used for good educational purposes, individuals and groups may also use it with other aims in mind. There is no simple answer to this. However, an aid to guarding against abuse is incorporating a clear value-base, such as the philosophy of co-development, and encouragement and willingness to ask difficult questions about how far the ideals are in fact guiding leadership practice.

The final challenge discussed was that of feasibility, where concerns about the practicality and logic of leadership distribution were raised. Traditional hierarchical leadership is often accepted and appears more comforting because of concerns about the efficiency and effectiveness of the alternative. These misgivings are to a significant degree countered by the potential for benefits examined in Chapter 2. It was suggested in that chapter that there is sufficient evidence from a range of studies of and experience in the practice of leadership distribution to indicate that investment of time and resources into its development is likely to be worthwhile – with the qualification that any benefits of leadership distribution do not occur automatically but tend to be associated with certain factors: strong co-ordination and planning, a cohesive culture, a clear focus on the organisation's core purpose, development of people's leadership capabilities and effective internal accountability.

In our judgement, the capacity and confidence to facilitate and benefit from collaborative leadership distribution can be fostered throughout a school. Vital to the success of such an enterprise, however, is the development of a robust conception of leadership that understands what leadership is and what it needs to be for and that addresses critical questions of purpose, self and power. In Chapters 4 and 5, we articulate a conception of collaborative leadership that, we argue, provides the required robust understanding.

4

INTENTIONALITY AND EMERGENCE

Chapter structure

- Introduction
- Intentionality
- Emergence
- The relationship between intentionality and emergence
- Summary

Introduction

The previous chapter outlined some challenging issues for the idea and practice of leadership distribution. In this and the next chapter we elaborate our conception of collaborative leadership, by explaining its essential propositions:

- the two lenses of intentionality and emergence (Chapter 4)
- the integration of a philosophy of co-development (Chapter 5)

This view of collaborative leadership is intended to maintain what is valuable in the idea of distributed leadership and address its limitations.

The first proposition says something about critically important features concerning the nature of leadership. It addresses the question: 'What is leadership?'. This first proposition is that leadership needs to be viewed through the two lenses of intentionality and emergence, so that we are better able to explore both issues of agency and power on the one hand and the complexities of change on the other. This chapter concentrates on the first proposition, explaining in turn the two lenses of intentionality and emergence, then considering the relationship between the two.

The second proposition, discussed in Chapter 5, proposes a way of encapsulating what is of greatest significance in defining the purpose and values of leadership practice and in making leadership worthwhile. It addresses the question: 'What should leadership be?'. Intentionality is guided by concerns and values which the person holds important and, however imperfectly or vaguely, by a sense or assumption of what is morally worthwhile. Our argument is that core values of democracy and social justice are essential measures of intentionality and the leadership that emerges from ongoing actions and interactions. These core values are encapsulated in what we describe as a philosophy of co-development. This philosophy takes the view that people have an innate potential for holistic and ethical growth and self-direction that is best nurtured through collaborative activity and mutual respect. The philosophy of co-development contrasts with the philosophy of dependence which we associated in Chapter 2 with a privileging of hierarchical leadership.

Intentionality

Intentionality is the conscious deliberation and willingness that give rise to leadership actions and interactions. People as agents of action initiate and guide practice and express meaning, purpose and goals. For example, a teacher, Sarah, notices that some children arrive at school apparently hungry. She talks with one or two of them and finds that they are not having breakfast before coming to school. Sarah talks to the deputy headteacher and asks if she can start a Breakfast Club, providing tea and toast. The Parent–Teacher Association subsidise the club and Sarah gets the support of colleagues who take turns in making the tea and toast and talking with the children. In this example, the series of actions originates in Sarah's intentionality and is shaped by others' intentionalities, including the deputy headteacher and members of the Parent–Teacher Association.

Recognising intentionality allows us to examine the different ways in which it may be expressed. It encourages us to consider, for example, who has the capability to turn intentions successfully into actions, and what accounts for variations in this capability. Is it down to personal factors, or are there social and organisational factors that affect this? Similarly, it encourages us to consider what kinds of intentions are encouraged or hindered. Which ideas for action and change are valued, which are not, and why?

Sarah's intentions are not explained in the example above. However, they appear to arise from a desire to nurture young people and perhaps an understanding of the connection between physical well-being and learning. Such intentions are nurtured by the school community. Sarah is given both permission to act and collegial and resource-based support to achieve her aims.

We can distinguish between different variables concerning the formulation and expression of intentionality – specifically its source, level in an organisation, its social character and the kind of personal reflexivity associated with it. These are summarised in Figure 4.1.

Intentionality occurs as the product of group encounters and formal meetings, as well as arising from individual reflection and deliberation. It arises from individuals in designated senior leader posts and from those at subordinate levels in the organisational hierarchy as they go about their everyday actions and interactions. The social character of the processes through which intentionalities arise and are given effect can differ, however. Intentionality can be the product of communications up and down a hierarchy and the subsequent formulation of a decision by the senior leader, to be passed down a hierarchical chain of command. It can also be the product of a process of open discussion in a climate that encourages free expression and debate, and a participatory procedure of decision-making.

source	• individuals
	• groups, teams or formal meetings
level	• senior leadership, at the highest levels of formal authority
	• people at other levels in the organisational hierarchy
social character	• hierarchical: top-down direction and instruction concerning the purpose of the group or organisation's activity, in accordance with traditional, hierarchical leadership
	• participatory: the conscious, collaborative, democratic creation of purpose through participative dialogue
personal character	• traditional reflexivity
	• critical reflexivity

Figure 4.1 Variables relating to intentionality

The personal character of intentionality – and the type of agency a person is able to enact – can differ too. The discussion of different kinds of intentionality is continued in Chapter 5 in relation to critical and traditional reflexivity, with a particular focus on critical intentionality. It is discussed there because the significance and worth we attach to critical intentionality arises from the value-base (the philosophy of co-development) that we argue is integral to collaborative leadership. We explain that critical intentionality is associated with relational freedom and pro-active agency and involves a greater degree of critical rather than traditional reflexivity.

Our argument is that intentionality should not be submerged and lost in the necessary appreciation of leadership as an emergent process. Indeed, the complex processes of interaction, which we discuss in the next section in relation to complexity theory and emergence, do not make sense if people's intentions and agency are not explicitly recognised. Intentionality is an integral part of emergence and infuses distributed processes of leadership.[1] Without the specific recognition of intentionality, there is a danger that, whilst appreciation of leadership as an emergent process grows, the importance of the personal capacity for conscious initiation of action may be overlooked.

Emergence

The second lens is emergence. From this viewpoint, we see leadership emerging from numerous, ongoing actions and interactions. Many organisational actors initiate, influence and co-create change, the outcome of which forges the character and direction of the organisation. Thus the nature and direction of organisational life arise from the perpetual interplay of people, ideas, social structures, artefacts, environmental conditions and relationships. This interplay can be studied to understand or illuminate why an organisation is like it is, rather than other possible forms or cultures it might have become. Whilst there are patterns and continuities in organisational life and outcomes, intentionality, particularly where critical reflexivity is employed, opens possibilities for change and innovation. At the same time, influence is not equally open to all. Some actors are more influential and powerful than others. Some structures are more constraining than others.

Theories of complexity and distributed leadership inform this second lens, as well as research that approaches leadership from a practice perspective. Complexity theory fosters a keen appreciation of the uncertainty that is a characteristic of the complicated and ongoing processes of action and interaction that make up organisations (Boulton et al., 2015). The features and outcomes of organisational life emerge from local interactions. The nub of the complexity is that while 'individuals can plan their own actions, they cannot plan the actions of others and so cannot plan the interplay of plans and actions or plan and control population-wide "outcomes"' (Stacey, 2012: 18). The implications of this challenge for leadership and for senior leaders have been explored by numerous writers such as Griffin (2002) and Flinn and Mowles (2014). Kevin Flinn and Christopher Mowles (2014: 2) note that 'complexity perspectives have been taken up ... in scholarship and teaching about leadership with leadership development providers such as Ashridge Business School, Roffey Park, Harvard Business School, and the Leadership Foundation for Higher Education (Leadership Foundation), incorporating aspects of complexity theory into their programmes'. Common to conceptualisations of leadership as an emergent, complex phenomenon is that 'they broadly conceive of organizations not as top-down structures

---

1 Hawkins and James (2017) highlight the intentionality of interactions in complexity theory.

of rational control, but as loosely coupled systems, networks or processes of learning and collective knowledge creation that devolve autonomy to agency at all levels': instead of relying on senior figures who drive change, 'leadership and change agency become identified with the systemic self-organization of learning by broadening leadership theory to encompass participative models of learning across the whole organization' (Caldwell, 2006: 2).

Complexity theory recognises that emergent systems can give rise both to desirable and undesirable organisational features, to democracy as compared with dictatorship for example (Stacey, 2012). In addition, organisational and system structures are not comprised only of the official forms sanctioned or striven for by senior leadership and policy-makers. They can for example, include opposing ideas and values, expressed as counter cultures.

Leadership-as-practice (L-A-P) is another and more recent way of articulating an understanding of leadership as emergent and complex. The L-A-P perspective proposes that leadership can only be understood by focusing on the practice that gives rise to it. L-A-P is 'less about what one person thinks or does and more about what people may accomplish together. It is thus concerned with how leadership emerges and unfolds through day-to-day experience' (Raelin, 2016a: 3). Joe Raelin (2016a: 3) argues that this view may invert 'our traditional views of leadership' as it

> does not rely on the attributes of individuals, nor does it focus on the dyadic relationship between leaders and followers, which historically has been the starting point for any discussion of leadership. Rather, it depicts immanent collective action emerging from mutual, discursive, sometimes recurring and sometimes evolving patterns in the moment and over time among those engaged in practice.

This resonates strongly with the notion of distributed leadership. The idea of distributed leadership goes back at least to Cecil Gibb (1968), as Peter Gronn (2002) identifies. Gibb argued that leadership should be seen 'as an interactional phenomenon that is an outcome of group dynamics, and not necessarily the action of the person or persons who are designated as having leadership or management authority' (Woods and Woods [G.J.], 2013: 3). Alma Harris and John DeFlaminis (2016: 141) summarise the core of distributed leadership as its emphasis on 'leadership as practice rather than leadership as role or responsibility' and on 'interactions rather than actions'; 'leadership is not simply restricted to those with formal leadership roles but … influence and agency are widely shared'. If these elements are understood to have benefits, an evaluative definition of distributed leadership encompasses certain implications for practice. Philip and Glenys Woods constructed such an evaluative definition – 'applied distributed leadership'. They suggest that it captures the view of distributed leadership that fires the interest of policy-makers and practitioners and has stimulated much research orientated to school improvement in the current policy context. Applied distributed leadership (Woods, 2015a: 177; Woods and Woods [G. J.], 2013: 4) involves a school culture that

- views leadership as emerging from ongoing flows of interactions across the organisation and its hierarchy, not simply the actions of the single leader or small leadership elite
- values leadership contributions from across the organisation and its hierarchy
- recognises that this view of leadership can be deployed in order to improve organisational effectiveness.

Such a culture is accompanied by institutional structures that

- spread leadership opportunities beyond formal senior roles to enable different sources of expertise and perspectives to influence the organisation's work, development and innovative changes
- facilitate flexible, collaborative working relationships across traditional boundaries and hierarchies
- tend towards the creation of flatter hierarchies.

Critical reflections in Chapter 2 threw light on important limitations of distributed leadership in this applied form. Issues raised from this critical perspective are the extent to which such leadership serves economistic and performative aims, promotes a constricted view of learning and fails to address power inequalities and social injustices.

It is clear that understanding organisations and leadership as complex phenomena does not mean that the idea, and reality, of hierarchy become irrelevant. Both hierarchy and emergence are present in organisations. The persistent paradigm of top-down hierarchical leadership cannot be ignored. At the same time, the emergent conception of leadership offers an understanding of the fluid nature of hierarchy and how its effects are conditioned by the swirl of everyday interactions. The 'top-downess' of leadership becomes a different notion when immersed in an organisation that consciously understands and seeks to work with the concept of leadership as fluid and emergent. Where an organisation takes the latter approach, enabling people across the organisation to enhance their everyday activity as contributors to leadership or co-leaders, greater recognition is given to the variety of forms of intentionality, shown in Figure 4.1. The importance of other forms of intentionality is recognised and valued, with 'top-downess' located as one amongst multiple forms of intentionality.

The vignette below, concerning an initiative in Latvia, shows how such fluid and emergent leadership can impact professional learning. The development agenda is set not by the headteacher but by the teachers themselves; their intentionality is recognised as a valid precursor to action, alongside the intentionalities of those in formal leadership positions. We highlight here particularly how certain features, such as mutual trust and teacher development, are not the products simply of leadership actions: they arise from the co-operative kinds of interaction taking place between teachers.

Since 2005, Broceni Secondary School, in the Broceni district of Latvia, has worked as an Innovative Experience School (IES). Such schools aim to improve the quality of student learning through teacher development. Teachers collaborate within and across schools, taking part in activities such as open lessons and professional development workshops. Teachers have worked to move from a critical response to peers to a more appreciative recognition of success. Whilst not all teachers are keen to participate, those who do take part feel that these opportunities to build teachers' knowledge, skills and understanding through mutual trust and space for co-operation lead both to teacher development and a beneficial learning culture for students.

(The vignette is based on case study L1a from the EFFeCT project – Roberts et al., 2017.)

From the complexity perspective, however, understanding complexity theory does not provide a route to re-asserting a more subtle and effective top-down, linear process of senior leadership control, should this be desired. The complex process of organisational life identified by complexity theory '… cannot be "cracked once and for all" and "engineered" by a policy maker or another "spectacular" leader endowed with godlike insight and power' (Bates, 2016: 12). There is no 'secret formula' which enables senior leaders to re-assert a linear process of control in the face of complexity. The point remains that organisational and system-wide coherence emerges from local 'rules', or 'local organising principles' that influence local interactions (Stacey, 2012: 14). These principles are the norms, rules or legitimate scripts that guide the practices and relationships of an organisation.

A good example of the complex process of organisational life can be found in the story of Newley School in England (Roberts, 2005). Designated a failing school by the then Office of Standards for Education, Children's Services and Skills (OFSTED), the school leaders attempted to put in place a package of measures to move the school forward. However, the OFSTED categorisation prompted all staff to reflect on their potential role in the school's recovery process. Many, unsurprisingly, decided to move on to promoted posts in other schools. This coincided with a national recruitment crisis which meant that many posts at Newley were filled by temporary staff, with a high proportion of permanent staff teaching outside of their subject area. Many students resented this situation and behaved in disruptive ways. Staff were overstretched and so were not able to put the new policies into action. The recovery of the school was therefore not achieved and it finally closed. The recovery of Newley School clearly could not be engineered by a process of linear, senior leadership control. The agency of other actors came into play in a national and local context not of the leaders' control and which did not allow the clear plans to be effected.

If senior leaders cannot act as 'godlike' actors seeing the organisation or system from the outside, what is the nature of their role? One of the suggested implications is that senior leaders have to step back from their traditional power and authority, as we noted in Chapter 2 (Harris, 2012; Woods, 2005). Gratton draws attention to the fact that the kind of organisational space and relationships that give rise to intense, energetic, creative environments – which she calls hot spots – cannot be deliberately created or 'manufactured' by fiat of the leader. But there are possibilities, she argues, for leveraging change to maximise the opportunity for hot spots to emerge. Such institutional levers include targeted funding, such as bonuses as incentives and the provision of communication technology, or cultural levers, such as setting the priorities and modelling values (e.g. valuing diversity and co-operative relationships). The role of senior leaders is not expunged by understanding leadership as emergent. Different patterns of leadership involve varying degrees of hierarchy and degrees of both directive and distributed leadership, giving rise to the idea of hybrid leadership (Day et al., 2009; Gronn, 2009). The role of senior leaders is a matter that requires addressing more fully in distributed leadership cultures. We do not consider that it is a matter of evolving from a simple top-down model of leadership to a more sophisticated conception of senior, positional leaders as background manipulators who enact change by finding and shifting the right levers of change. The latter is too mechanical as a metaphor. Our understanding of the role of senior leaders is set within the later discussion of leadership as a reciprocal learning relationship (see Chapter 6) and exploration in later chapters of the active role in nurturing collaborative leadership of both non-positional and positional agents of change across the school.

The relationship between intentionality and emergence

In our terms, intentionality is embedded in the process of emergence. Our embracing of intentionality and emergence accepts both the agency of people and the ongoing flow of interactions and their emergent outcomes as real contributors to leadership. The dual character of leadership being an organisational or social product and a product of human agency underlies the twin lenses of emergence and intentionality.

In recent years, tendencies to bring together personal leadership and the distributed character of leadership are more easily discernible in the distributed leadership literature. Peter Gronn, having led the wave of interest in distributed leadership, has developed a significant degree of scepticism about its value. For Gronn most recently, distributed leadership provides only part of the story of leadership.

There is a spectrum of possibilities from individual leadership, such as the dictator, to collective leadership or leadership by a group. In other words, there are various configurations of leadership that involve greater or lesser degrees of individual and collective leadership. Scholars of distributed leadership have to be absolutely clear about what they are analysing and 'get an ontological grip on the unit of leadership analysis', otherwise it is 'time to abandon ship' (i.e. abandon distributed leadership), Gronn (2016: 5) argues. He goes on to propose that the unit of analysis is the 'spectrum of possibilities' between the two poles of individual and collective leadership (2016: 2). The attraction of this hybrid notion of leadership can be seen in other work. Research concerned to advance social justice has advocated 'a combination of superhero/collaborative leadership' (Capper and Young, 2014: 162; see also Theoharis and Causton, 2014).

An important study by Meng Tian and colleagues has led to their proposing a resource-agency duality model of distributed leadership. Leadership as resource refers to the interaction between actors and artefacts/situations which 'determines both the emergence and the nature of the resource'. Leadership as agency is about actors having ownership, empowerment, self-efficacy and well-being and involves 'individual-social dualism' – that is, a recognition that agency requires the social or organisational opportunity to exercise it. An understanding of both is required to understand leadership according to Tian et al. (2016: 157–158).

The lenses of intentionality and emergence affirm the orientation of these approaches, but also provide what we feel is a more fruitful conceptual framework. They offer a different way of responding to the challenge of the unit of analysis, raised by Gronn. David Hartley (2009: 147) argues that there is a tension in the research by Jim Spillane on distributed leadership. Although the purported focus is practice and the interactions that occur, in fact in Spillane's approach 'the individual still retains ontological status'. Through the identification of intentionality, we explicitly acknowledge the importance – the ontological status – of the individual when conceiving leadership as a distributed phenomenon.

Our lenses therefore recognise different and important aspects of the leadership process: the thinking and feeling activity of people, the intentionality that drives their agency and the different forms and levels through which intentionality is generated, as well as the complex processes underpinning social stability and change indicated by theories of emergence and complexity. In Tian et al.'s resource-agency model, the resource aspect denotes the importance of interaction and the relevance of all the non-human factors (artefacts, structures and so on) that contribute to leadership. We believe that viewing this as emergence more clearly situates that lens in the wealth of insights arising from complexity theories, emergence and the distributive character of leadership. Our focus on intentionality relates to agency and emphasises the importance of the formulation and expression of meaning, purpose and goals and the conscious deliberation involved in leadership.

The lenses of intentionality and emergence help us engage with three issues important for leadership practice. The first is the paradox of power and complexity. Although we experience power in organisations, the complexity of organisations and distributed leadership suggests that no one person is able to direct change. Recognising intentionality, we can see that influence and power can be exercised through intentional actions at various levels. These include intentionality that leads to top-down direction and instruction in the form of traditional, hierarchical leadership. Such actions may or may not have the consequences intended: that is what we learn from complexity theory. But there can nonetheless be real and significant consequences when actions are taken by someone who is able to utilise greater resources, of authority or finance, than others. Influence and power can also be exercised by individuals and groups from different organisational levels and spaces and in different ways (see Figure 4.1) as a result of formulating their own purposes and intentionalities. Thus, influence and power – for good or ill – can be exercised in micro-level interactions by those exercising non-positional leadership as well as from positions of formal authority.

The second issue is the different ways in which clarity of direction in organisations emerges. For some organisations, an unclear direction and purpose leads to a perception of the need for clear leadership. There is a lack of coherence, which organisational members may experience as confusion, low morale, disillusion, and so on. In other organisations, there is a coherent strategy and clear direction of travel. Both scenarios are a consequence of the interplay of people's intentionalities and organisational structures. Both organisations are led, but the leadership is giving rise to different consequences. Where coherence and a sense of a shared direction of travel is experienced, this is due to an alignment between the various intentionalities within the organisation so they generate a momentum with a common orientation.

The third issue is the nature of knowledge and knowledge creation. Viewing leadership through the lenses of intentionality and emergence has implications for our understanding of the relationship between knowledge and practice. People's interpretation of the world is bound up with the ongoing processes of interaction from which stability and change emerge. People use and are influenced by the ideas and values in the organisation's culture but they do not simply apply them in a mechanical manner. To a greater or lesser degree, they deliberate upon and interpret them. Critical intentionality, which is discussed in the following chapter, involves a greater degree of deliberation and choice-making than intentionality that is shaped by traditional reflexivity, and that includes reflecting on and shaping and formulating knowledge. Two points are apparent then. The first is that intentionality is a creative, knowledge shaping process. The second point follows from recognising that knowledge is not simply applied *to* practice. Ideas and knowledge are also created and shaped through practice. Here we can draw on the insights of practice studies and 'knowing in practice' (Gherardi, 2016). The practice of people as they interrelate with other people, artefacts and their environments results in the creation or emergence of knowledge. Practice – itself an emergent feature of numerous interactions – helps generate knowledge and thereby feeds into intentionality.

Summary

In Chapter 1 we summarised the basic concept of leadership as referring to the influences, arising from human intentions and actions, that make a difference to what a group or organisation does – its direction, goals, culture, practice – and how it is seen and experienced by those who work in or relate to the group or organisation. In the current chapter we have elaborated the first of the two propositions which conceptualise collaborative leadership. This first proposition says something of critical importance about the nature of leadership – what it is. It was argued that leadership needs to be viewed through the two lenses of intentionality and emergence, so that we are better able to explore both issues of agency and power on the one hand and the complexities of change on the other. Intentionality refers to the motivation and meaning, the conscious deliberation about such things as purpose and priorities, and the formulation of the will that gives rise to leadership actions. Emergence recognises that the totality of leadership influences is the product of numerous, ongoing interactions involving many organisational actors: the nature and direction of organisational life arise from the perpetual interplay of people, ideas, social structures, artefacts, environmental conditions and relationships.

The chapter also explained the relationship between intentionality and emergence. In the complex processes of practice intentionality is embedded in emergence. We argued that nevertheless it is important to distinguish the two. The two lenses give explicit recognition to different and important aspects of the leadership process: on the one hand, the thinking and feeling activity of people, the intentionality that drives their agency and the different forms and levels through which intentionality is generated, and on the other the ongoing processes underpinning social stability and change indicated by theories of emergence and complexity.

In the next chapter, we turn to the second proposition which concerns the values of leadership practice, addressing the question of 'What should leadership be?'.

5

Philosophy of Co-development

Introduction

This is the second of two chapters in which we elaborate our conception of collaborative leadership, by explaining its essential propositions:

- the two lenses of intentionality and emergence (Chapter 4)
- the integration of a philosophy of co-development (Chapter 5)

To restate briefly, the kernel of our argument is that leadership needs to integrate explicitly both people's agency and emergent social change, as well as explicit critical values. The argument is cast in the form of two propositions. Chapter 4 elaborated the first of these propositions: the need to understand leadership as the outcome both of people's intentions (intentionality) and the complex flow of interactions in the daily life of schools (emergence). In this chapter, the second proposition is addressed: the need to integrate values of democracy and social justice, encapsulated in a philosophy of co-development. If one takes the view that values of democratic participation and social justice are crucial to human living, leadership requires an articulated explication of and commitment to these values. Hence, the conceptualisation of collaborative leadership we are constructing is founded on a philosophy of co-development (Woods, 2016a), which encompasses the ideas of holistic democracy and an expansive view of social justice.

The need to elaborate values

Leadership inherently gives expression to values, either explicitly articulated or implicitly held. Intentionality inevitably involves an evaluation of possible actions based on a person's perspective on the concerns and ethical considerations that are most important to them. The culture in which leadership practice takes place and with which people interact encourages certain concerns and values and inhibits others. Any leadership approach, therefore, has to be critically examined from the perspective of the values it promotes, encourages or inhibits. Hence, any conceptualisation of leadership needs to give explicit and considered attention to its values position.

Simon Western's work on leadership is an important contribution to understanding what is involved in leadership as a distributed process and explores a growing leadership discourse (Western, 2008, 2013). He describes how this discourse of eco-leadership is emerging and how it can be placed in the context of successive waves of leadership discourses from the beginning of the twentieth century. First is the 'leader as controller' which assumes that leadership focuses on maximising efficiency and control to increase output. In the later 'leader as therapist' discourse the leadership task is assumed to be about human relations, the idea being that 'happy workers are more productive workers'. The emergence in the 1980s of the 'leader as Messiah' discourse followed an economic slump in the US. In this discourse, the vision of a transformational leader is used to drive strong, dynamic cultures, where control is achieved via peer and self surveillance, rather than hierarchical power or coercion. This has been and continues to be an enormously influential discourse. All of these discourses are versions of hierarchical leadership.

The eco-leadership discourse is very different. Western's account of eco-leadership sees it not simply as a functional change in leadership, in response to changing circumstances, but a leadership perspective that entails particular ethical and values stances. The workplace is seen 'as interconnected eco-systems', in which central control is obsolete. Eco-leadership focuses on connectivity and inter-dependence; it encourages distributed leadership at local levels, leadership from the edge and the building of strong networks, coalitions and collaborative relationships that are responsive and adaptive to change. These features are all vital to success.

Additionally, eco-leadership integrates a view of values and ethics that, according to Western, challenges and subverts the narrow logic of the market (Western, 2013: 258). This stance is not only about personal conduct but also addresses organisational and systemic issues. Eco-leadership is

> concerned with acting ethically in the human realm *and* protecting the natural environment. Systemic ethics goes beyond company values and individual leader morality, which conveniently turns a blind eye to the wider ethical implications of their businesses, e.g. by ignoring social inequality, the downstream impacts of pollution and supply chain workers, world poverty and environmental sustainability. (Western, 2013: 254)

Eco-leadership values what Western terms 'leadership spirit', which means to draw from the spring that we all have and 'from which the human spirit and ethics flow'. Recognising this source is vital to extending 'values beyond material gain', paying attention to 'community and friendship' and to 'the unconscious and non-rational, creativity and imagination', and drawing upon the beauty and vitality within human relationships and the natural world (Western, 2013: 254).

An example in education of the discourse Western is commending is the work by Lisa Kensler and Cynthia Uline on leadership for green schools. They put values at the centre of this leadership. Their work shows that green school leaders who 'ground their practice in ecological and democratic principles cultivate the conditions in which students' well-being is high and [students] engage more deeply in meaningful learning' and that leadership for green schools not only helps restore the ecosystem but contributes 'to improving communities' (Kensler and Uline, 2017: 176).

This articulation of eco-leadership reinforces and encourages our case for the integration of a critical values orientation in leadership, which we formulate as a philosophy of co-development. Such value-based leadership is exemplified in the story of Elsa Prendergast who strove to develop a struggling school into a learning haven (Ehrensal, 2016). Despite its children coming from a disadvantaged neighbourhood, the school eventually provided a strong environment for learning, in which individuals were valued and community cohesion was strong. Elsa's leadership was grounded in democratic and ethical values. Acknowledging the community's particular needs, she worked with parents to understand their issues and to resolve them together. Her leadership approach allowed for the development of an ethic of justice at the school, with the right of all children to a good education acknowledged and acted upon. Elsa described her leadership style in terms which strongly resonate with collaborative leadership.

There is some overlap too with distributed leadership. However, it is important to be clear on differences between much in the distributed leadership field and concepts such as collaborative leadership and eco-leadership. Whilst overlapping the latter concepts in many ways, the field of distributed leadership has given insufficient critical attention to questions of values and where it places itself in relation to issues of ethical purpose and social justice. Much of the field is framed within school effectiveness and improvement concerns as defined by dominant policy discourses. The critiques of distributed leadership discussed in Chapter 3 were focused on issues of purpose, self and power, one of the prominent critiques of distributed leadership being its harnessing to marketising and performative agendas that narrow educational purpose (Hall et al., 2013; Hammersley-Fletcher and Strain, 2011; Woods and Woods [G.J.], 2013). Critical research on distributed leadership offers a challenging perspective on the kind of autonomy being created by leadership distribution. The charge is that this autonomous agency allows individuals discretion to act in ways consistent with a self that is defined by the values and priorities of neo-liberal, competitive governance, measured by narrow calculations of achievement. Thus distributed leadership can be seen as a mechanism for controlling organisational members' identities and behaviour.

The conceptualisation of distributed leadership is weakened where it fails to address the issues of purpose, self and power. To address this requires the integration of an explicit evaluative element, open to scrutiny and debate, into leadership conceptualisation to complement the descriptive element (intentionality and emergence) (see Chapter 3).

Over a decade ago, a relationship between distributed leadership and social justice was identified by England's National College for School Leadership:

> Distributed leadership provides fertile ground for maintaining long-term commitments to the desired goals of equity. Achieving equitable outcomes for all learners is beyond the capacity of individual highly talented leaders and requires the knowledge and expertise of others in the school working with a shared sense of purpose. Formal leaders, no matter how talented, cannot make the equity agenda thrive without leadership coming from others in the school. (National College for School Leadership, 2004: 3)

However, an articulated and considered view of what constitutes the values of social justice is needed for a leadership approach to have a chance of making a substantial difference to inequities and experiences of injustice. If values of social justice and democratic participation are taken to be crucial to life and society, leadership conceived as a distributed process with implications for practice has to embrace these values. To address the weakness exposed by critical reflections on distributed leadership, the conceptualisation of leadership we are constructing is founded on a philosophy of co-development that comprises a rich conception of democratic values, which we articulate as holistic democracy, and an expansive conception of social justice (Woods, 2016a). From the perspective of this philosophy, as noted in Chapter 1, we learn and work best by supporting each other and by bringing together the different experiences, expertise and ideas that we have as a diversity of people in a group or organisation. Starting with holistic democracy, the components of the philosophy of co-development are now explained.

Holistic democracy

Central to the practice of holistic democracy is the opportunity for people to grow as whole persons, able to forge a meaningful life, and to participate in the co-creation of their social and organisational environment, in a climate that promotes mutual respect, critical dialogue, independent thinking and belonging. The purpose at the heart of holistic democracy is to enable people to develop a capacity for freedom as social beings. Hence, the notion of holistic democracy places value on both meaning and participation (Woods, 2011; Woods and Woods [G.J.], 2012).

The intellectual roots of holistic democracy lie in three ideas concerning the human capacity for learning and ethical development. Firstly, people possess an *individual potential for holistic growth* (including spiritual, ethical, intellectual and emotional capabilities). Holistic democracy incorporates the ideas of developmental democracy, reflecting people's capacity to nurture their 'innate potential excellence' (Norton, 1996: 62); each person has moral and spiritual faculties open to cultivation (Vincent and Plant, 1984). Secondly, people's *growth is a relational process*, not just a matter of individual effort. Holistic growth involves interacting, connecting and empathising with others and the world in which we live, and learning with and from other people. Moreover, it involves contributing to the well-being and growth of fellow human beings and the flourishing of our environment, which includes the natural world and the aesthetics of the built environment; it involves turning 'lovingly or caringly to what lies beyond oneself' (Dallmayr, 2007: 65). Thirdly, to enable individual growth and relational processes to thrive, people cannot be reduced to dependent followers of requirements and ways of life forced upon them, but *need to be co-creators of the social and ideas environments* in which they live. The more people actively work together in co-constructing aims, values, ideas and how to live and work, the more likely it is that they and their environments will flourish. Hence, holistic democracy encourages collaborative learning and reflects the aims of deliberative democracy.

This concept of holistic democracy is elaborated through four interrelated dimensions which are ideal-typical representations of what it means to practise holistic democracy (Woods, 2011, 2017b). The first two – holistic learning and relational well-being – concern the creation of meaningful lives, a process that is integral to holistic-democratic participation. These are explained below.

Meaning dimensions of holistic democracy

Holistic learning. This is about the pursuit of truth and meaning. It encapsulates the idea that a key purpose of the practice of democratic leadership is to work towards as true an understanding as possible, not only of technical and scientific matters but also questions of enduring values, meaning and purpose. This is pursued as a guiding aim, rather than a final destination to be achieved, through the development of all our human capabilities (spiritual, cognitive, aesthetic, affective, ethical, physical) and by learning collaboratively. As Gidley (2017: 255, original emphases) puts it in her exposition of postformal learning, learning requires 'an integration of the search for *truth* – via scientific and philosophical epistemologies; with *beauty* – via artistic/aesthetic sensibilities; and with *goodness* – via participatory embodiment and critical enactment of the truth claims that we profess'.

Relational well-being. This is about connectedness that nurtures the best of our humanity. It involves feeling empowered and developing high self-esteem as a member of communities (such as communities of practice as well as an organisation in which a shared identity with others is enjoyed) – in a social environment that values the capacity to think for oneself (the criticality of critical reflexivity) and where there is a sense of belonging and a deep relatedness to other people, the natural world and those things that feed the human spirit. The kind of belonging characteristic of relational well-being is one in which communities and organisations are supportive, practice shared responsibility for the work and its consequences, create fertile conditions for pro-active agency, and form authentic social bonds where 'participants remain freely open to their own possibilities' (Dallmayr, 2016: 50). It is founded in the open social environment discussed in Chapter 8.

The second two dimensions are the participative dimensions of holistic democracy and are explained in the box below.

Participative dimensions of holistic democracy

Power sharing. This concerns active involvement in shaping the institutions, culture and relationships that make up our social and organisational context and having a say in decisions that affect us. It entails discretion to act freely, take initiatives and express identity – that is, pro-active agency – within the parameters of agreed values and responsibilities. It may include exercising formal rights to participate in decision making and in choosing and holding power-holders to account.

Transforming dialogue. This is the practice of exchanging and exploring views and engaging in open debate to reach beyond individual narrow perspectives and interests and enhance mutual understanding, seeking out the greater good for everyone. Mutual respect, openness to listening to others' viewpoints and the sharing of constructive critique are crucial features in this. In such dialogue, aspirations to holistic learning are tested and knowledge and aesthetic, ethical and spiritual sensibilities, enhanced.

Social justice

Integral to holistic democratic practice is an expansive notion of social justice (see Figure 5.1) (Woods, 2012; Woods and Roberts, 2013a). The notion is an expansive one because it incorporates distinct factors of crucial importance to people's quality of life and learning. How these factors are differently experienced and how they are distributed has profound implications. Social justice is thus sketched as a four-fold scheme. It is constructed from the three-fold typology set out by Alan Cribb and Sharon Gewirtz (2003): participative, cultural and distributive justice. Participative justice concerns people's rights to participate in the decisions which affect them. Cultural justice is concerned with the absence of cultural domination, lack of recognition and disrespect. Distributive justice focuses attention on eradicating unjustified socio-economic inequalities and deprivation, which in education includes access to the material supports of learning such as IT, books and digital resources.

To these we have added developmental justice. This is concerned with factors that facilitate or hinder growth as a person and the development of a person's knowledge and capabilities. It reflects a philosophical position that values the nurturing of holistic growth as articulated in the notion of holistic democracy. Inequalities in exposure to factors that facilitate and hinder learning affect the development of capabilities which enable a person 'to do things he or she has reason to value' (Sen, 2009: 231). Such inequalities create difficulties in achieving a 'human rights imperative for all people to have a reasonable opportunity to develop their capacities and to participate fully in society' (Levin, 2003: 5).

type of social justice	focus	goal to lessen inequalities in ...
developmental justice	learning	... opportunities and support for learning and holistic growth
participative justice	participation	... opportunities and support to have a voice and contribute to decisions that affect you
cultural justice	respect	... respect and recognition of cultural differences
distributive justice	resources	... unjustified socio-economic inequalities and their negative effects

Figure 5.1 Four-fold scheme of social justice

Critical intentionality

In a study that we undertook of a school with a well-developed culture of distributed leadership, the sense of *pro-active agency* that many teachers and some support staff felt was palpable (Woods and Roberts, 2016). Participants were clear that the school was one in which pro-active agency was both valued and supported. One participant captured this in describing the school as having an 'opportunity culture' (Woods and Roberts, 2013b: 23):

> The more you engage, the more you tend to enjoy because you are more open to opportunities and if you are not open to opportunities how do you know if it is going to be a good one?

Teacher-initiated projects were encouraged and supported through a Teacher Led Development Work Group (Woods and Roberts, 2016) which all members of staff were invited to join. A middle leader in the school saw this group as indicative of a culture which encourages creative and collaborative thinking and action.

Pro-active agency is exhibited in the way this group works. If agency is conceived as a general capability to think, feel and act,[1] pro-active agency is the enactment of change and purposeful innovation grounded in feelings of sufficient confidence and conviction to initiate and carry through, individually and with others, such change. Pro-active agency is part of leadership which is understood as 'the process whereby teachers can clarify their values, develop personal visions of improved practice and then act strategically to set in motion processes where colleagues are drawn into activities such as self-evaluation and innovation' (Frost and Roberts, 2011: 10–11). Collaborative leadership entails pro-active agency that aspires to reflect in practice the values of holistic democracy and social justice and nurtures relational freedom.

From the discussion of intentionality in Chapter 4, it is clear that there are numerous and varied intentionalities forged every day. The intentionality we are interested in exploring in this section builds on the key place of pro-active agency in leadership distribution. We suggest that the intentionality that is associated with pro-active agency is characterised by *critical reflexivity*. Margaret Archer argues that there is a particular imperative in contemporary times to develop 'powers of reflexivity' in order to formulate courses of action in novel and fast-changing circumstances (Archer, 2012: 1). A more intensive reflexivity is becoming prevalent and necessary. There is a lack of old scripts and rules to follow as the varieties of organisations, products and new ideas increase exponentially. The mode of intentionality needed in such circumstances is one that

---

1 There has been an immense amount of writing in the field of sociology on agency. This definition is a simple one for our purpose and is consistent with Archer's analytical dualism on which the trialectic process (see Chapter 8) is based. Extensive discussions of agency are in Archer's work – e.g. Archer, 1995 (such as pages 149–154), 2000 and 2003 (beginning with the opening discussion on page 1) – where further references may be found. For a view challenging Archer and other sociologists writing on structure and agency, see Holmwood (2014).

is both self-critical and critically evaluative of social action. Archer (2012: 32–45) calls this meta-reflexivity.

Work by Lynda Gratton, developed over more than a decade predominantly in the business field, carries a sustained argument about the changing nature of organisations and leadership. Her observations of how organisations work and innovate led to conceptualising a new phenomenon of hot spots, which we first encountered in the previous chapter. These are

> not amenable to the old rules of command and control, under which employees are told what to do and then rewarded for their actions. In the new rules of Hot Spots, rather than be commanded, employees choose to develop important relationships with others, and rather than be controlled, they actively choose to make their time available to this collective sense of purpose. (Gratton, 2007: 146)

Gratton argues that organisational members are less attracted to being dependent and to leadership and work practices that reflect, in our terms, the assumptions of a philosophy of dependence. Dependence, and hierarchal leadership, nevertheless still hold attractions, as we noted in the discussion of the 'heroic' leader model in Chapter 3. However, Gratton's point is similar to that of Margaret Archer: social and organisational contexts and structures are changing in ways that draw many people to adopt a different approach to how they think about and live their social lives. More critical reflection and choice-making are involved as innovation and changes in organisational boundaries, cultures, services and products increase exponentially. Hot spots, occurring in the context of dissolving traditional organisational boundaries, involve 'boundary spanning' across categories of people, across new or enduring functional divisions and across organisations. Shifting structural contexts and boundaries such as these create the imperative for critical reflexivity and pro-active agency.

In contrast to critical reflexivity is *traditional reflexivity*, a form of reflexivity which we argue is characteristic of intentionality less conducive to change and pro-active agency. Here, the individual's intention and agency are shaped by organisational need or the imperative to follow others. This is similar to Margaret Archer's concept of communicative reflexivity in which the person's deliberations need to be confirmed and completed by others; communicative reflexivity is conducive to stability and keeping personal deliberations framed within 'local custom and practice' (Archer, 2012: 33). We might further suggest that traditional reflexivity is more likely to be associated with a philosophy of dependence – that is, the view that people are fundamentally dependent on being directed and provided with instructions and definitive guidance in order to know what to do. This is not an absolute relationship. Traditional reflexivity can involve some degree of independent thinking. However, we suggest that traditional reflexivity is more likely to involve a mindset consistent with a philosophy of dependence.

Intentionality is the precursor to an individual initiating action. Intentionality that involves traditional reflexivity is predisposed to keep things as they are; or at least to make decisions that reinforce tendencies, based on fear or inertia rather than any moral purpose, to slow down change. On the other hand, intentionality that involves critical reflexivity orientates teachers and others to becoming pro-active agents of change, free of – or at least more distanced from – a restricting philosophy of dependence. In studying cases of teacher leadership and collabora-tion, we have found that initiation – by which we mean the impetus that begins and generates change informed by critical reflexivity – is important. This idea of initiation is integral to teacher leadership in action. In accounts we have studied by teachers engaged in teacher leadership, it was notable that the teachers

> did not simply contribute to the implementation of an idea which had its genesis with school leaders. Instead, they designed their own approach to solving a prob-lem they personally saw as an issue and, in so doing, demonstrated a high level of participative professionalism. (Woods et al., 2016: 6)

The vignette below demonstrates this intentionality in action. It focuses on Gertie who, at the time she wrote the story, was a teacher in a middle school in England and wished to develop boys' enthusiasm for writing.

Gertie was determined to find a strategy which would result in enhanced enthusi-asm and interest in writing for the boys in her class and might also influence whole school policy and practice in supporting writing development. She formed a work-ing group with six boys with varying writing abilities who would help her develop alternative approaches to supporting their writing. The boys thrived in the collab-orative environment of this working group, providing exciting ideas which Gertie incorporated into her schemes of work. The working group members agreed that children need to have a purpose for their writing and this set the direction for the new activities.

The impact of this change in approach was considerable, with the boys now showing a much more positive response to writing activities and developing enhanced writing skills. Noticing the impact which a collaborative approach had on the pupils, Gertie continued to meet with the working group on a regular basis. They worked with her to evaluate lessons, to design activities for forthcoming les-sons and to decide together how learning objectives could be achieved in exciting and innovative ways.

Gertie was amazed by the levels of maturity demonstrated by pupils, by their fantastic suggestions and by the dramatic impact which her new approach was having on pupils' attainment. The working group decided to ask all the other children for feedback about approaches to teaching writing. They gave out post-it notes and asked their peers to indicate the benefits of the new approach to developing writing.

(Continued)

At this stage in the project, a children's author and poet, Wes Magee, was visiting the school and he led a workshop with Gertie's class. Together they created a poem. The children asked if it could be published in Wes Magee's next book but the author explained it wasn't his poem, it belonged to the class. The class therefore decided to produce their own book in which to publish their writing. Gertie discussed this idea with the senior leaders in her school and got a very enthusiastic response. The previously reluctant-to-write boys set up a writing workshop to produce material for the book. This idea excited the pupils so much that they immediately began to write with publication in mind. Some even created stories at home in their spare time in the hope that they would be published in the class book.

(The vignette is an abridged version of Bustard, 2012.)

Intentionality is apparent in Gertie's initiation of the project, as she enacts a non-positional teacher leadership role. It is manifest in her aim, her determination, and in the way she resolved to approach the project. Other forms and sources of intentionality are also evident and crucial to the trajectory the project takes. For example, the children felt that they wished to publish their poem and expressed the desire to do this. They then found a way forward when their initial idea was rejected.

At the same time, this story cannot be understood simply as a series of enacted intentions. Gertie and the children's steering of the project emerge through a distributed, interactive process. For example, the boys' positive response to writing activities is given further effect by Gertie noticing this and deciding to continue working with the working group. This in turn gives rise to an originally unanticipated participation of other children, and then the engagement with the visiting poet, in response to which the idea and practice of creating a published class book arises. The process and direction of the project recounted in this story are the product of myriad individual and group interactions, intertwined with expressed and enacted intentions.

The project has a values-orientation, concerned with social justice and participation. The philosophy of co-development can be used as a framework to examine the story. Some of its key principles are apparent, for example. The project arises from a determination to address the lower achievement of boys in writing, in Gertie's class and, then, through the involvement of others, across the school – that is, to address developmental injustice (see Figure 5.1). The creation of a working environment that reshapes the top-down authority relationship between teacher and students is integral to the working group's culture and practice. The mode of practice is collaborative, as the group and Gertie decide together how learning objectives could be achieved, reflecting the values of power sharing and transforming dialogue.

Such critical intentionality involves a high degree of what Gert Biesta terms subjectification – that is, developing as an individual with a capability to think and act independently of the communities into which the person is socialised. Socialisation leads to belonging – becoming a member of 'particular social, cultural and political "orders"' – in the way that a person becomes a member of the teaching profession or a school community (Biesta, 2009: 40). Subjectification is not inconsistent with belonging in that it is about 'ways of being in which the individual is not simply a "specimen" of a more encompassing order' but has their own sense of intentionality and agency (Biesta, 2009: 40). This individual is able to think for themselves, exercise critical reflexivity and be part of an organisational and professional community with a sense of belonging.

We would say that this individual is able to exercise freedom. We are referring here to social and relational freedom, rather than a conception of an unfettered free will, able to do anything it may conceive. Relational freedom is freedom as a social individual, which develops through processes of individual and relational learning over time: it is about learning how and in what direction to develop one's own individuality and one's own social identity and practice, learning with and from, as well as contributing to the well-being of, others. It may be described as 'freedom with others' (Butler and Athanasiou, 2013: 183). There are degrees of such freedom. It may develop and increase (or indeed lessen at times) during a person's lifetime; it may differ between people. Relational freedom involves being able to exercise self-control, which includes moral responsibility, so rather than passive application of ethical rules, relational freedom requires deliberation, sensitivity and a willingness to explore and take a view on ethical matters. The key factor is the degree to which the person is able to arrive at their own decisions informed by a considered awareness of themselves and the context of which they are part – including its opportunities, resources, constraints and ethical demands.

The deliberations and reflexivity of intentionality and the capacity to engage in critical reflexivity are crucial factors in the nurturing of relational freedom. (For discussions of freedom, see Baggini, 2015; Dallmayr, 2016; and Woods, 2017a.) Let us summarise, then, what we mean by critical reflexivity. It is characterised by:

- enhanced personal capabilities for reflection and deliberation and an intensified sense of the need and desirability for making choices and devising innovative practices and policies

- commitment to seek in practice expression of the values of holistic democracy and social justice and to nurture relational freedom.

Such critical reflexivity is a vital ingredient in the critical intentionality that is essential to collaborative leadership.

The two vignettes which follow illustrate intentionalities characterised by subjectification, relational freedom and collaborative activity. They show critical reflexivity in seeking to devise practical changes that will advance social justice. The first, an initiative in Hungary, emphasises how individual and collaborative intentionalities were focused on achieving maximum impact.

Two years ago, The Foundation for Democratic Youth (DIA) in Hungary initiated a project, *DeMo*, for civil society organisations to network, learn together and share experiences and knowledge. The thirteen organisations that participated all work with children who live in extreme poverty, often studying in segregated institutions characterised by lower-quality education. The organisations participating in the project use different methods and strategies to fulfil the common aim of compensating for the deficiencies in formal education in an attempt to close the social gap between the majority and minority, disadvantaged, marginalised social groups.

The *DeMo* project involved the organisations working collaboratively to support their professional development and to ensure the maximum impact for their work. Flexibility was key to the success of the project, with project members enabled to take the initiative to change agendas and the direction of meetings to suit their developing needs. A participative, democratic model of professionalism was clearly evidenced in this case study. Facilitating the agency of participants, who would then come to their own solutions to personally meaningful issues, was found to be the most productive way of working. Rita Galambos, DIA director, conceptualised her role as a leader of the network through the metaphor of a spider making a web. The spider is not in the centre, or outside: it has the function of slowly connecting the little parts and constructing the web that holds everyone together.

(The vignette is based on case study H1 from the EFFeCT project – Roberts et al., 2017.)

The next vignette is about Merita who, at the time of its writing, was a teacher in Macedonia. It shows relational freedom in action and elements of the project and its collaborative leadership can be related to values of holistic democracy and social justice. Merita's critical intentionality is apparent in her initiation of the project which did not rely on a formal position within the school, and in the impetus for the project which is deeply embedded in a commitment to social justice, especially cultural and participative justice (see Figure 5.1). Others within the project also demonstrate their own critical intentionality, working alongside Merita to ensure that the project had an impact within their own setting. The collaborative mode of practice is apparent, with Merita working with colleagues to determine both the shape of the project and its supporting structures. The process and outcomes of the project illustrate progress towards dimensions of holistic democracy: transforming dialogue through language acquisition that aided communication and co-operation; holistic learning (see Figure 5.1) in the awareness-raising about culture and introduction of multi-cultural education; and relational well-being (see Figure 5.1) in the greater integration and cohesion that resulted.

Merita's school serves a multi-ethnic community which includes Albanian, Macedonian, Turkish and Roma families, all with different cultural traditions, language and religion. Merita wanted to help to overcome prejudice, improve intercultural communication and foster tolerance between different ethnic communities. She decided to devise a series of workshops to help people to learn the Albanian language, offered as an elective subject in her school. She devised a series of workshops for teachers, school principals and other educational professionals from the different ethnic groups.

Around 20 participants took part in the initial workshops, designed not only to teach the Albanian language but also to raise awareness of the culture in the hope that participants may then be able to include the teaching of Albanian in their own schools. The workshops had a very positive impact, with Albanian now being taught in other schools. However, the most important impact of the project was the integration it promoted.

Merita decided to extend this work, becoming project co-ordinator of the IIEP project which focuses on inter-ethnic integration within schools. She continued to work with her colleagues in the four schools under the banner of 'Overcoming prejudices by learning the language of the others'. The aim was to enable teachers to become familiar with the languages spoken by all students within their schools and to facilitate peer-to-peer learning. Students taught each other their language, fostering familiarity, tolerance and mutual respect.

The impact of this work has been dramatic. Not only has it led to a rich pattern of language learning and multi-cultural education, it has also changed the structure of educational provision within these schools. Previously taught separately, students are now routinely taught in multi-ethnic groups. This is having a massive impact not only on the way the school operates but also on the community which is experiencing more social cohesion than was ever thought possible.

(The vignette is an abridged version of Sejdini, 2014.)

A values framework to aid critical reflexivity

The concepts and core values of holistic democracy and social justice constitute a challenging values framework which can be used to reflect on and seek ways of improving leadership practice. This values framework builds into the notion of leadership as a distinct ethical commitment to a specific set of values that aids critical intentionality in leadership practice. We have used these concepts as a basis for critical questions that are offered in the final section of Chapters 9 and 10, and for catalysts for reflection and change in Chapter 11.

In essence, the concepts of holistic democracy and social justice are intended to be helpful in focusing attention on two areas in relation to leadership practice. The first is *inclusive participation*, so that the voices of all are heard and valued. This involves dialogue that is open, respects differences and seeks to learn from others and find constructive ways of tackling challenges. Leadership practice that promotes inclusive participation is also prepared to ask critical questions systematically and continually about who has fewer opportunities, whether based on racial, sexual, cultural or other forms of discrimination that work against equity. A concern is to work towards the eradication of discrimination and unfair power differences that mean that some people are unable to participate and be heard, are not given respect, are economically deprived and are blocked from developing their full capabilities. The absence of these kinds of discrimination and inequalities promotes inclusive, holistic learning.

The second area is *holistic growth*, anchoring distributed leadership in a framework of deep learning. Learning framed in this way develops cognitive and emotional abilities, skills for employment, ethical, aesthetic and spiritual capabilities, an understanding of democratic citizenship and appreciation of values such as justice and tolerance, as well as fostering the ability to reflect and learn continually throughout life. Leadership practice for holistic growth works to create a social environment in which relationships are supportive and encourage independent thinking as well as a sense of belonging and shared commitment.

Summary

This chapter has argued for and set out the second of the two propositions which elaborate our view of collaborative leadership. The second proposition is that there is a need to integrate an explicit evaluative element, open to scrutiny and debate, into leadership conceptualisation to complement the descriptive element (intentionality and emergence), and that this should be based on the values of a philosophy of co-development.

This philosophy incorporates the ideals of holistic democracy – that is, the creation of opportunities for people to grow as whole persons, able to forge a meaningful life, and to participate in the co-creation of their social and organisational environment, in a climate that promotes mutual respect, critical dialogue, independent thinking and belonging. At the heart of holistic democracy is a commitment to people cultivating a capacity for freedom as social beings – relational freedom. Integral to holistic democratic practice is an expansive notion of social justice that is concerned to tackle inequalities in learning, participation, respect and resources. The integration of a philosophy of co-development into leadership builds in a commitment to a specific set of values and offers a challenging framework to aid critical reflexivity in and on leadership practice. This framework can be summarised at its simplest as an imperative to focus attention on efforts to improve leadership in two areas: inclusive participation and holistic growth.

The elaboration of the two propositions in Chapters 4 and 5 is intended to provide an understanding of collaborative leadership that is analytically robust, incorporating a critical understanding of distributed leadership, and ethically explicit. We would like to conclude with a neat diagram that shows the key ideas and their relationships in our argument. Such a diagram, however, runs the risk of implying that leadership practice can be a tidy and highly organised process. The diagram in Figure 5.2 instead attempts to convey the messiness and complexity that overlay and subsume the conceptualisation of leadership as expressed through the lenses of intentionality and emergence and the philosophy of co-development which encompasses the holistic-democratic values and social justice. (Later – in Chapter 11 – we succumb to the temptation to present a much neater diagram.)

Figure 5.2 Collaborative school leadership: Concepts and messiness

In the following chapter we continue with key themes of holistic democracy – learning and power relations. We explore collaborative leadership as a reciprocal learning relationship involving all those who are engaged in non-positional or positional leadership, and relate this to the complex interaction and negotiation of multiple authorities within landscapes of leadership practice.

6

LEADERSHIP AS A RECIPROCAL LEARNING RELATIONSHIP

Chapter structure

- Introduction
- Leadership as reciprocal learning
- Multiple authorities
- Landscape of leadership practice
- Summary

Introduction

This chapter takes a journey which leads to an exploration of collaborative leadership as a reciprocal learning relationship. It begins by discussing some of the issues concerning the role of positional leadership by senior leaders in a distributed leadership culture. These were foreshadowed in Chapter 4 where it was observed that the role of senior leaders is not expunged by understanding leadership as emergent.

This opening discussion leads into an explanation of the idea that leadership is a process of space-creation to facilitate the learning of those led by the leader. We do not accept, however, that a rigid distinction should be made between leader and led, with the latter's learning dependent on the former; so a radical reorientation to this idea is then proposed. It is argued that the learning facilitation entailed in leadership is neither one-way nor necessarily top-down; rather, such learning is reciprocal with a directional emphasis which can change according to circumstances. Collaborative leadership entails a reciprocal learning relationship: both non-positional and positional leaders in different ways contribute to leadership and fostering mutual learning. Just as leadership is distributed, so is the facilitation and fostering of learning.

We move on to argue that there are multiple kinds of authority in schools. We suggest these multiple authorities are sources of different kinds of knowledge and learning and reinforce the fact that learning is not necessarily one-way or top-down. It is then argued that the processes of leadership in a school can be viewed as occurring across a landscape of leadership practice, made up of numerous leadership practice communities.

Leadership as reciprocal learning

There are challenging questions concerning the nature of senior leadership in a more distributed culture. Is it fundamentally different from exercising senior leadership down a traditional hierarchy? In what way is it different? The discussions in previous chapters indicate that collaborative leadership does not necessarily replace senior, top-down authority, but works with and reframes its meaning.

From a complexity theory perspective, idealising the leader as a visionary change agent and concentrating on techniques of leadership obscure the real power of leadership and leadership development programmes in sustaining disciplinary power and the status quo of power and authority. What is needed is explicit, critical reflection on what leadership and techniques of leadership actually do and the raising of issues of 'power, difference and conflict': this is not on the grounds that all disciplinary power is bad, but because questioning and raised awareness help to increase understanding of what leadership is really doing and brings to the surface ethical issues (Stacey, 2012: 76–77).

Ralph Stacey makes the distinction between two forms of exercising power and influence. This first is described as *techniques of power*, which may have good or bad consequences. We see these as including practices such as ensuring tasks are allocated, setting up and operating ways of monitoring progress, explaining an organisation's or a project's aims to staff and identifying professional development needs. The second is described, following the work of Edgar Schein, as *coercive persuasion*. This is a practice that is specifically targeted as changing what people think, based on the notion that the senior leader knows what is good for the organisation. It 'seeks to foster dependency … and block reflexive thinking' (Stacey, 2012: 80). In our terms, coercive persuasion creates and advances a philosophy of dependence. Leaders who exercise coercive persuasion may seek to justify this in terms of the general or organisational good, but, argues Stacey, it is 'inimical to learning' (ibid.). Coercive persuasion involves powerful people intentionally changing the mindsets of others and blocking reflection and critical thinking, with the justification that resocialising people in this way makes them more suitable for and effective in their organisational roles.

The idea of coercive persuasion suggests that there is a contrasting phenomenon of *non-coercive persuasion*, a more benign process. This needs probing to establish what it means. We seek to understand the idea of non-coercive persuasion through an exploration of leadership as a pedagogical relationship. There are what we regard as positive, progressive attempts to encourage teachers and others to think differently about leadership. For example, in the story of Melissa Oyediwura (Chapter 2, in the section on innovation), the headteacher, Tracy, acted as a co-tutor of a group of teachers, encouraging all group members to think differently about leadership, to recognise their own capacity to lead the changes which resonated with their educational values. This kind of practice is justifiable on the grounds that there are good, ethical reasons for enabling teachers and others to enact proactive and collaborative leadership. What is crucial is that such practices actively encourage reflection and critical thinking, including engagement with challenging research and literature outside the local practice of the teachers concerned. Hence critical reflexivity is a crucial theme in later chapters. If the 'currently dominant ideology of leadership may make it feel natural to train people to apply the techniques of disciplinary power in an unreflexive way' (Stacey, 2012: 74), an implication is that considerably more explicit emphasis is required on critical reflection.

We suggest that the alternative to coercive persuasion is essentially leadership activity that fosters learning and critical reflexivity. We start by indicating how leadership is or can be a process that promotes self-development, critical reflexivity and the confidence and capacity for initiation, and thereby creative, pro-active agency – that is, a process that fosters learning. The work of Michael Uljens, building on a European pedagogical tradition, argues that the leadership relation between school leader and teacher is less about the individuals and the roles they occupy and more about the space (the relationship) between them. Moreover, it is about 'summoning' others – or, we might say, inviting others – to 'self-activity' (Uljens et al., 2016: 107). The leadership relationship from this point of view is about creating space in which the other is encouraged to actively engage in self-development and change. For Uljens, this conception of the leadership relationship is the same as that between teacher and student. Uljens uses the understanding of the pedagogical relationship in the classroom to illuminate leadership. A leader in relation to the teacher (or a teacher in relation to the student) focuses on the other as a constantly becoming subject, as someone involved in an ongoing process and interchange (Aspelin, 2014). Dialogue is a key part of this. Such dialogue involves 'the capability to create active trust through an appreciation of the integrity of the other' (Giddens, 1994: 116). It is also a challenging process that includes 'a search for shared meaning and common understanding', questioning 'taken-for-granted assumptions', collegial enquiry and the gathering of evidence (Frost et al., 2008: 4–5).

The point about leadership inherently being an activity which fosters learning in others was made by James MacGregor Burns in his seminal book on transformational leadership in the 1970s: 'Ultimately education and leadership shade into each other to become almost inseparable, but only when both are defined as the reciprocal raising of levels of motivation rather than indoctrination or coercion' (Burns, 1978: 448). Reciprocity is explicit in this quote, though in the rest of Burns' book the emphasis is on a one-way, top-down process – namely, the leader raising up followers. Our emphasis, by contrast, is on the leadership process as one of reciprocal learning. It is not necessarily the senior leader who 'summons' or invites the other person to self-development and learning. We are therefore viewing the learning inherent in leading as a 'co-constructivist' process (Rhodes and Brundrett, 2010: 155). More than this, the point we are making is that in a collaborative leadership culture, everyone may exercise pro-active agency and engage in initiation, and everyone might learn from others. Leadership as a co-constructed learning relationship is distributed. That is, who invites the other to self-activity and self-development depends on circumstances and the specific matters of concern. The knowledge and insights engendered by multiple authorities are negotiated, as we shall see in the next section.

We are proposing then that leadership constitutes a reciprocal learning relationship. Articulating it in this way brings to the fore a feature of the Carpe Vitam Leadership for Learning project which we mentioned in Chapter 2. The Leadership for Learning principles recognise that learning 'occurs in the flow of interaction among members of the learning community' and 'is enhanced through opportunities to exercise leadership' (Frost et al., 2008: 3). Leadership as a reciprocal learning process is best seen not so much as a series of discrete mutual exchanges but as a flow of interactivity.

Such a flow is clearly seen in the vignette about Amina Eltemamy below. The flow of leadership activity at a number of levels of both position and experience is clearly illustrated. Amina applies her critical intentionality to initiate a change and brings her learning about teacher-led development work to the new network she creates and her interactions with teachers; participants who learnt through their own experience in the first year of the programme applied their own critical intentionality to foster change by becoming sources of learning for their colleagues. Reciprocal learning – learning from one another through open and honest exchange (transforming dialogue) – is at the heart of the programme.

Amina Eltemamy, a former teacher, is a PhD student at the University of Cambridge, who was determined to use her studies not simply to examine a situation but to change it. The first part of her research focused on examining the views of a group

(Continued)

---

of teachers working in Egyptian schools about their profession. After attending a seminar about the HertsCam International Teacher Leadership programme she decided to introduce Teacher Led Development Work (TLDW) programmes in Egypt, to enable teachers to develop their professionality by leading development programmes which arose from their own values and concerns.

Amina began the CairoCam Network in 2014, as a network of four private schools. Amina worked with teachers in these schools to plan the programme together, adapting the HertsCam TLDW programme to their local context.

Many participants were nervous about taking the initiative to lead change and required much support. In the second year of the programme, some of this support was provided by the previous year's participants who passed on their learning to their colleagues.

The networking element of this project was particularly important. The teachers had the new experience of leading their own conference, of learning from one another rather than from external speakers. Teachers' comments demonstrated the inspirational power of such an event, where open and honest exchange of stories can lead to deep and reciprocal learning.

The published story of Amina's work is also being used within the wider HertsCam Network to inspire teachers in the UK to take up the challenge of individual and system reform.

(The vignette is adapted from Eltemamy, 2017.)

Learning as an integral feature of leadership relations reflects the second of the intellectual roots of holistic democracy highlighted in Chapter 5: that human growth is a relational process. Such learning is relational or reciprocal in two senses. Firstly, a person – student, teacher, member of the support staff, parent, and so on – can facilitate learning in others or learn from others at different times according to circumstances. Knowledge is passed between people. Secondly, people can learn together as they work and share ideas and reflections and jointly generate new knowledge and understanding. They co-construct their learning. This second aspect of reciprocity is the more dynamic and creative process, in which more emerges from the interactions than simply the sum of what individuals bring. The learning is emergent.

The learning we are referring to is not solely cognitive or only about developing skills and techniques. It is holistic in the sense discussed in Chapter 5. It concerns emotional, social, aesthetic and ethical growth. In so far as the transforming leadership advocated by Burns involves reciprocal learning, it 'ultimately becomes *moral* in that it raises the level of human conduct and ethical aspirations of both leader and led, and thus has a transforming effect on both' (Wren, 1998: 146).

Our crucial caveat to this is that who is leader and who is led depends on circumstances and the matters at hand, not simply organisational position. There are many practical instances of this in teacher-led projects in England.

In a teacher-led project on language, for example, 'the students and teacher shifted their role from learner and imparter of knowledge to co-learners' (Woods et al., 2016: 10). Another teacher who was part of a Teacher Led Development Work group explains a collage that they created as part of a project on collaborative teacher learning (Woods et al., 2016: 21):

> We put our roots down, we suck up all that knowledge and learning and we add to the layers and then we branch out in our different ways but they all intertwine. So although my project was yoga it came from doing some training in another subject and then listening to what people said about children's attention being lower so sometimes the ideas don't just come from me they come from lots of other things.

Leadership as a process of reciprocal learning is integral to the principles of teacher leadership in the network in which these teacher-led projects take place – for example, cultivating moral purpose (rather than imposing ethical competencies), enabling professional development through design and leadership of projects, nurturing learning communities and critical friendships, enabling critical reflection and dialogic activities, and facilitating the use of discursive and conceptual tools and fostering mutual inspiration (Woods et al., 2016: 29).

Multiple authorities

Leadership as a relationship of reciprocal learning raises questions of expertise and authority. Who has, or should be accorded, authority concerning a particular area of concern or question of practice? In relation to this, the recognition that there are multiple authorities is helpful (Woods, 2016b).

Our view of authority is wider than the Weberian view which sees it as the legitimation of top-down control. This is just one form of authority and one way of achieving co-ordination in social and organisational life. There are other ways and other forms of authority that are not about domination. Following the discussion of power and authority in Woods (2016b), some forms of authority may legitimate top-down power – power over others; but others may legitimate power-with – shared and co-operative power 'through and with others' (Blackmore, 1999: 161).

The idea of multiple authorities is based on the notion that there are different legitimacies that may constitute a basis to be respected, listened to and influenced by. Authority is not something that is held or taken. It is granted by or co-constructed with others through acceptance that the power or influence that someone exerts is legitimate. This granting or according of authority we refer to as *authorisation*. It emphasises that authority is not a static attribute, but is the ongoing outcome of a process that occurs between people. The distribution of authorities may therefore shift and be subject to re-assessments and reallocations by people in day-to-day interactions.

Different authorities may be held and deployed by different people across a school. So, for example, some may have a specific or outstanding professional expertise in teaching or in another area, such as technology, finance or management; some may be able to carry a charismatic authority through their force of personality; some may commend a change in a school's policy as something required to respond to competitor schools – in other words, as a change that carries with it the authority of the market; some may have experiential authority through the kinds of experience they have had, such as dealing with the challenges of running a closing school or of schools merging, or experience in engaging classes of highly disaffected students. Some of the authorities likely to be apparent in schools are shown in Figure 6.1.[1]

formal	bureaucratic, legal-rational authority in which the holder of a post has authority in a hierarchy of posts
professional expertise	rational authority based on claims to knowledge and capabilities gained through recognised programmes of education and training and command of a body of knowledge
experiential	an acknowledged authoritative character which a person gains through their personal and/or professional history and the responses and actions they have gone through in facing challenges
charismatic	authority accorded to a person because of some special characteristic they have or their force of personality
traditional	authority distributed according to communally legitimised criteria such as gender, ethnicity, age or social class
democratic	authority of a person and the decisions and actions they enact gained through the legitimacy given by an accepted process of participation, dialogue and consent
market	authority for decisions and actions being carried out derived from the legitimacy accorded to the forces of competition and the perceived need to respond to these

Figure 6.1 Types of authority

These different authorities have influence only if they are seen as legitimate. Claims to authority may be contested. Where authority is perceived to exist, there are opportunities for enabling learning. Knowledge that gives rise to professional or experiential authority for example, or which is held as part of traditional authorities, is a resource.

---

1   See Woods (2016b) for further discussion.

We do not assume these multiple authorities to be sources for a simple, one-way process of transmitting knowledge and learning from the authorised to another. Apart from anything else, the claimed or implied authority requires critical reflection by others who may augment, adapt and contest the ideas and knowledge any authority source may offer. Rather, the different authorities are diverse starting points for leadership to create spaces for reciprocal learning. These starting points are distributed across the school population according to where these authorities are or develop, and can occur equally amongst non-positional and positional leaders.

For example, a newly qualified teacher who, let us say, has developed an understanding of innovative practices in a certain aspect of teaching – and hence gained a degree of professional authority in that aspect – takes the initiative and applies their knowledge. The teacher engages in initiation using the new and distinctive professional expertise they have gained, introducing a new practice in their classroom. That is one way they express leadership, by intentionally bringing about change that affects students. *In addition*, that teacher engages in leadership by facilitating learning amongst colleagues by creating spaces for them to engage in self-activity and self-development concerning the innovative practice and the knowledge-base (such as research literature) around it. This is not by getting them to learn what the newly qualified teacher knows. Rather, it is encouraging colleagues to engage with this new knowledge and to bring their experience and expertise to bear on that knowledge so that they develop their own understanding. For senior leaders, the learning may well be around how to encourage and support both future innovation and knowledge-sharing.

To close this section, we provide an illustration of authority that is collaboratively constructed and shared from a case generated by a European project on collaborative teacher learning. The case is about a peer observation of teaching programme (POT) (Roberts et al., 2017). The programme has been set up across Mary Immaculate College (MIC) situated in Limerick, Ireland, and the University of Limerick (UL). In this programme, lecturers support their peers through a process of collaborative learning through lesson observation and feedback. Lecturers meet to plan the focus of the observation, they then observe their partner's lesson and subsequently offer reflections to stimulate mutual learning.

Lecturer commentary on the POT indicates it is perceived as a conduit for collaborative learning. This collaborative learning is strengthened through the structure of the POT, where the lecturer being observed determines who their observer will be and the timing and focus of the observation. The training provided facilitates an understanding of the process and the degree to which adaptations and changes are appropriate. In this way the process supports deep learning through being to some degree individually bespoke.

Landscape of leadership practice

The idea that there are multiple authorities interconnecting and being shared and negotiated in numerous interactions throughout a school steers us to imagine what it is like to look across the school and these knots of interactions. It draws us to consider the concept of 'landscape of practice', which consists of 'a complex system of communities of practice and the boundaries between them' (Wenger-Trayner et al., 2015: 13). The processes of leadership in a school can be viewed as occurring across such a landscape of leadership practice, made up of numerous leadership practice communities. Hence, as well as there being multiple authorities, a school is made up of multiple communities of leadership practice which interact and overlap with each other.

Examples of communities of leadership practice include a senior leadership team and their interactions, with middle leaders, teachers and others. The senior leadership practice would typically be widespread across and beyond the school. Another example could be a teacher-led group developing innovative practice. Such a group might involve teachers, support staff and perhaps students. Its spread in the school landscape would be smaller, but there could be some interaction and overlap with the senior leadership practice through, for example, interaction with a particular senior leader. A further example could be a student-led group in which a small group of students are taking the initiative on an agreed area of activity. This could be the development and maintenance of a school garden, or giving feedback on an aspect of the curriculum. Roberts and Nash (2009) investigate the impact which groups of students, working in partnership with teachers, can have on the school improvement process. Multiple impacts – for example, on students' self-view and agency and student–teacher relationships – demonstrate how a community of leadership practice can strongly influence the leadership landscape of a school.

Communities of leadership practice are sites and sources of leadership across the school. To illuminate what this means, we highlight three aspects of what occurs in their day-to-day practice using the concepts of intentionality and authorisation.

Firstly, communities of leadership practice are areas in which intentionalities and initiatives are developed and enacted. The patterns of intentionality in different communities of leadership practice are likely to vary in ways suggested by the variables in Figure 4.1 (Chapter 4). For example, all will have individual intentionalities, but some may have greater opportunities than others for group-led intentionality with a participatory character.

Secondly, such communities are constructed through the diverse intentionalities enacted in schools. For example, whilst one school may already have many consciously developed communities of leadership practice, another school may be developing and growing such communities. In the latter school, encouragement and facilitation may come from senior leadership. It may also come from actions and interactions by active or embryonic communities of leadership practice – that is, the communities' own intentionality and enactment of that intentionality.

Thirdly, communities of leadership practice are networks in which authorisations are formed and take place. They are sites where different authorities are deployed and created – formal, professional, experiential and so on. For example, a community of practice centred on the senior leadership team possesses a strong degree of formal authority. Teacher-led groups may gain their influence through professional expertise. It is important, however, not to over-simplify the authority characterising different communities of leadership practice. Multiple authorities will occur in all such communities, including varying mixes of experiential, charismatic, traditional and democratic authorities.

Activities by and between different communities of leadership practice are one way in which we can understand how leadership change is not solely a product of top-down senior leadership action. The idea of a landscape of leadership practice also encourages us to recognise the complexity and diversity of leadership change. The leadership landscapes of schools differ significantly. Hence the processes of leadership change are likely to differ. The numbers of communities of leadership practice, the variations and ongoing interactions between them and the multiple authorities that characterise them indicate the levels of potential complexity of a school's leadership landscape.

Whilst senior leaders undoubtedly exercise significant authority and influence, the multiplicity of authorities and communities of practice reinforces a view that developing collaborative leadership does not follow in a straightforward process from initiatives emanating from senior positional roles. Rather, it is important to understand that collaborative leadership development occurs through and as a product of leadership practised as a reciprocal learning process, which is discursively and collectively created over time across the landscape of leadership actors and practices in a school. The role of senior, positional leadership is discussed further in the context of non-positional leadership in Chapter 9.

Summary

This chapter has argued that collaborative leadership entails reciprocal learning relationships and is a dynamic pedagogical process. Since leadership is a distributed, emergent phenomenon, both non-positional and positional leaders in different ways contribute to leadership and fostering mutual learning. Collaborative leadership practice involves nurturing and expanding opportunities for fostering leadership as reciprocal learning across the school. Learning as an integral feature of leadership is reciprocal in two senses: it means facilitating learning in others or learning from others at different times according to circumstances; it also means learning together and jointly generating and co-constructing new knowledge and understanding. The learning we are referring to is not solely cognitive or only about developing skills and techniques, but is holistic, embracing emotional, social, aesthetic and ethical growth.

Where does the authority source for learning lie? It was argued that there are multiple kinds of authority in schools. These multiple authorities are sources of different kinds of knowledge and learning and reinforce the fact that learning is not necessarily one-way or top-down. It was argued that, as well as there being multiple authorities, a school is made up of multiple communities of leadership practice which interact and overlap with each other and form a landscape of leadership practice. Seeing the school as a landscape of leadership practice shows how intentionalities and actions arise from different sources of leadership practice across the school. The numbers of such communities, as well as their variations, interactions and multiple authorities reinforce the complexity of each school's leadership landscape and the impact which this can have on student and staff learning. An implication from this is the importance of recognising that collaborative leadership development occurs through and as a product of leadership practised as a reciprocal learning process, which is discursively and collectively created over time across the landscape of leadership actors and practices in a school.

Following the discussion in this chapter of leadership as reciprocal learning, in the next chapter we set out a learning model to support the development of collaborative leadership.

7

A LEARNING MODEL OF LEADERSHIP DEVELOPMENT

Introduction

What is involved in developing collaborative leadership in schools? In this chapter we explain the importance of a learning model of change to support such development. This model constitutes the day-to-day operation of leadership as a reciprocal learning process. It informs the remaining chapters of the book, where we focus on its implications for leadership understanding and practice.

The learning model contrasts with a *transmission model* of developing leadership change in schools – for example, through tools, techniques, procedures, formulas and the faithful application of best practice. Such a transmission model fits more easily with a mechanical view of learning, in which achieving the right combination of components and the planned application of initiatives will lead – albeit through potentially complicated processes – to certain ends. In leadership development, such a transmission model often demands a focus on the 'transfer of learning (learn now and apply later)' from the expert to the learner (Denyer and Turnbull James, 2016: 277), together with the accumulation of required competences. Leadership development approaches driven by such competency frameworks can too often fragment learning about leadership, reducing it to the mastery of techniques or procedures and the gaining of separate skills or attitudes that fail to address the needs of leadership practice in living, complex contexts. (See for example Denyer and Turnbull James, 2016: 263; Stacey, 2012: 107.) This is not to say that leadership does not entail the development of certain kinds of capabilities such as the capacity for awareness and learning and other skills, behaviours and attitudes that the person draws upon and applies creatively. Indeed, we discuss the need for such capabilities in Chapters 2 and 10. Our point is to emphasise the limiting nature of framing leadership development as competency-based.

Knowing in practice

By contrast, we emphasise the importance of framing the fostering of collaborative leadership within a *learning model* of leadership development. Such a learning model nurtures leadership through participants' questioning, problem-solving and application of creative responses in leadership practice. The learning model reflects what has been found concerning change and development in a number of fields of study and practice. For example, research in the field of interprofessional working confronts challenges similar to furthering leadership distribution, such as collaboration across traditional boundaries and the need to create new practices and changes in professional identity. Such research emphasises that the development of collaborative practice across professional boundaries is inherently a learning process, in which the guide is not an ideal model but is better characterised as an ongoing activity that involves finding out as you go along. Such a journey is inevitably accompanied by 'tensions and difficulties as well as insights and innovations' (Puonti, 2004: 10). The learning process perspective is informed by activity theory (Warmington et al., 2004) and includes the creation of new knowledge which transforms the activity and horizontal learning across competing and complementary domains. Yrjö Engeström puts forward the concept of 'expansive learning', or 'radical exploration', as a way of describing the learning involved in going beyond given, pre-existing activity.

> Radical exploration is learning what is not yet there. It is creation of new knowledge and new practices for a newly emerging activity, that is, learning embedded in and constitutive of qualitative transformation of the entire activity system. (Engeström, 2004: 15)

Developing collaborative leadership is a transformational process, by which we mean it requires change in people and across a system – be it, for example, a school, department, group or network. It is more than a change in individual leaders or would-be leaders and goes beyond the areas where leadership literature 'has invested significant time and attention' such as the qualities, behaviours and intelligences of leaders (Carroll et al., 2008: 372). It involves changes in culture, relationships, values and institutional structures, which we discuss further in Chapters 9 and 10. From the leadership-as-practice perspective, highlighted in Chapter 4, leadership development needs to be consistent with leadership being not the individualistic product of a leader but 'co-constructed through acts, activities, and interactions embedded in the situation in which it takes place' (Denyer and Turnbull James, 2016: 279).

The implications of an understanding of leadership as emergent and complex are relevant to developing collaborative leadership. The development of such leadership is ambitious. It requires developing leadership amongst those in both non-positional and positional roles, so that it is practised with an awareness of its distributed and emergent character and the vitality of diverse individual and shared intentionalities. Its practice similarly entails a commitment to values of democracy and social justice, encompassed in the philosophy of co-development.

Such a process has to take into account the insights of complexity theory. Jean Boulton et al. (2015: 232), discussing the implications of complexity theory, explain that open communication and questioning are key to trying out new practices and learning from them.

> Strategy [we could say leadership development] is not a blueprint or plan. [It is] an ongoing, unfolding, and emergent process. We … need experiments to test out possibilities, and we … need to allow for challenge, encourage diverse thinking, and above all make sure we are getting plenty of feedback so we can make adjustments on the way.

This echoes Engeström's (2004: 15) suggestion that 'forward-oriented expansive learning actions are intertwined with horizontal or sideways movement across competing or complementary domains and activity systems'.

The learning model of leadership development reinforces what was also indicated in Chapter 4: that leadership as a distributed process, characterised by intentionality and emergence, involves knowing in practice. As the field of practice studies indicates, knowledge – and intentions that arise from the knowledge a person has or gains – is not simply applied in practice (Gherardi, 2016). Instead, knowing is created in and through the practice of individuals as they interrelate with other people, artefacts and their environments. Thus people's explicit and tacit knowledge, a dimension of their intentionality, is formed by their practice, as much as by new knowledge or awareness from professional development activities such as studying and so on. If it is to be improved, practice requires critical thinking and problem-solving, which involves the generation of creative responses and is 'intrinsic both to the development of knowledge and to the formation of the self' (Holmwood, 2014: 16). Learning is inherent in fruitful practice development.

Wenger's theorisation of communities of practice illustrates the conception of learning which, we argue, underpins the learning model of development. Such learning 'cannot be designed. Ultimately, it belongs to the realm of experience and practice. It follows the negotiation of meaning; it moves on its own terms' (Wenger, 1998: 225). Moreover, the learning that we believe is essential for developing collaborative leadership involves critical reflexivity, a key aspect of critical intentionality and pro-active agency discussed in Chapter 4. Critical reflexivity is, to draw on Carroll's (2015: 94) distinction, more than self-reflection in which we attempt to work out why we have thought and acted in the ways we have; it asks hard and testing questions about our leadership practice to 'uncover our assumptions, limits and blind-spots in our ordinary reflection in relation to the politics, ethics and structures and the larger realities of our organizations, communities and societies'.

Collaborative learning

Integral to learning is the need to make it visible. In work on professional knowledge-building that we have been involved in, supporting others in making visible what they are doing is key to learning (Roberts, 2011). However, much practice, and the thinking behind that practice, is invisible (Perkins, 2003). Polanyi's (1966) discussion of tacit versus explicit knowledge focuses on the highly personal nature of tacit knowledge, deeply rooted in an individual's actions and experiences, their 'know-how' and in their embraced values. It is not easy to express. Explicit knowledge, conversely, can be more easily transmitted. It can be expressed in words or numbers and captured in records. Support is needed therefore to both reveal what is tacitly known and consider its applicability to other contexts.

The professional knowledge-building project referred to in the previous paragraph concerned the introduction of 'good practice' between schools in which teachers took a clear leadership role (Roberts, 2011). Reflection (Fielding et al., 2005) was positioned as central to the revelatory process of making learning visible and surfacing teachers' taken-for-granted practice. This reflection was intended to help teachers to challenge the simple idea that good practice could be transferred and to support them in systematically and critically assessing practice. Teachers 'de-coded' the practice they saw in order to identify what they had learnt from it. To facilitate this, teachers were offered a thinking routine developed by David Perkins and his team at Harvard University (Perkins, 2003). The routine can be summarised as:

Connect: How are the ideas and information connected to what you know already?

Extend: What new ideas did you get that extend your thinking in new directions?

Challenge: What is still challenging or confusing for you? What questions or puzzles have been raised?

The thinking routine encouraged teachers to connect actively with what they were seeing, to engage in purposeful and sustained reflection on what it might mean and how they might use it in their own practice. Perkin's routine seemed to be an example of Tabberer's (2003) description of knowledge management as a process which makes available people's knowledge about what works, so that colleagues can use it. In some ways, such routines appear fairly straightforward to enact. Arian Ward's view, quoted in Collison and Parcell (2004: 16), is more challenging however.

> It's not about creating an encyclopaedia that captures everything that anybody ever knew. Rather, it's about keeping track of those who know the recipe, and nurturing the culture and the technology that will get them talking.

Lessons from the project included the importance of representing new knowledge so it can be shared with others and the significance of connections between individuals. One of the conclusions was that active and ongoing processes of 'stimulating connections' – through which existing networks and communities are broken down, new ones created and staff encouraged 'to think beyond their normal circles of influence' – are vital ingredients of a school's capacity for learning (Collison and Parcell, 2004: 172).

Connectivity is one of the key variables that studies in complexity theory suggest significantly affects innovation and learning in organisations. Connectivity here refers to the pattern and intensity of relationships and communication between organisational members, especially across traditional boundaries (McElroy, 2010: 108; Seel, 2006). Leadership as a reciprocal learning relationship benefits from such connectivity and stimulating connections, as does the process of nurturing collaborative leadership.

So, is connectivity a key condition that can be brought into being by perceptive senior leaders? If knowing in practice, and learning and innovation, can be enhanced through increased connectivity, the implication would seem to be the need to find the right variables to manipulate in order to do that. What are the 'buttons to push' that will enable the learning to take place to develop collaborative leadership? Gratton (2007: 16), as we saw in Chapter 4, argues that senior leaders can encourage the 'emergence' of creative 'hot spots' through points of leverage – through subtle shifts in the structure, practices and processes of a company and the way decisions are made and resources allocated. Whilst not denying the importance of variables such as allocation of resources and changing organisational structures, the learning model pushes us to think about more than just creating the conditions of change or identifying levers of change. As complexity theory continually reminds us, change occurs not through the application of such neat, linear plans based on a mechanical or engineering perspective of change.[1]

It can help to think of intentional change, including the development of leadership, as 'facilitating emergence' (Seel, 2000: 6). Seel's notion of emergence is a normative one and is about innovation – new ways of working, new services or products and so on – that advances the purpose of the organisation, as contrasted with stable, repetitive patterns and outcomes. (Our concept of emergence, that we set out in Chapter 4, is an analytical concept; it is a way of understanding how society, organisations and leadership are the way they are. Stability and no change are emergent outcomes as much as change.) In relation to encouraging innovative emergence, Seel (2006) identifies a number of factors important in enabling change to emerge. These include connectivity, diversity of people, rate of information flow and intentionality and appear to be *pre-existing* conditional factors of innovative change. However, to see them like this would be to ignore the very thing that complexity highlights – the interconnectedness of variables and interactions which means that a simple linear account of enacting change falls short. Hence Seel's (2006: 9) discussion of the practical implications leads him to conclude that it is not a case simply of creating the necessary conditional factors, but to suggest that 'collaborative inquiry offers the best current approach to enabling and encouraging emergence in organisations'. Here the collaborative inquiry approach is not so much about leveraging change, by finding and shifting the right levers; rather it is about a process of continual shared discovery – that is, the knowing in practice highlighted above.

The learning model of leadership can be operationalised through shared processes of collaborative enquiry. Collaborative leadership learning groups (CLLGs) are one approach to facilitating and learning about collaboration and shared leadership practices (Denyer and Turnbull James, 2016). These are designed to provide a safe environment in which 'to explore the tensions, difficult experiences, and emotions involved in leadership' through the process of tackling practical problems. Participants take responsibility for what they intend to achieve and support each other's learning, alongside tutors who 'raise appropriate questions, highlight issues, supply relevant materials, and pay careful attention

---

1 We produced a 'toolset' (Woods and Roberts, 2015) for the purposes of a European project on school leadership, which as a first go in synthesising our conclusions about distributed leadership for equity and learning in that project may appear to promote, through its reference to key levers of change, a mechanical, linear approach to developing such leadership. This book is in part a fuller exploration and elaboration of the suggestions in that 'toolset' and explains the point more explicitly that leadership development is a complex process of critical and reflexive change.

to the dynamics of the group' (2016: 269). Participants draw on the experiential knowledge that they bring, as well as practical and theoretical public knowledge, such as research literature, and knowledge collaboratively constructed by the group (2016: 270).

An interesting example in education which focuses on how to sustain professional enquiry is the Critical Collaborative Professional Enquiry (CCPE) programme at the University of Stirling. In this programme, which attempts to change the culture and structure in which teachers work not just the capacity and knowledge skills of individuals, enquiry and learning become ongoing and integral parts of the organisational landscape. Data on CCPE suggest that the programme helps in enabling professional learning and practice to become sustainable; practitioners develop a view of professional learning as an emergent process in which practice comes to be the basis for creating knowledge and theorising (Drew et al., 2016).

There are clear similarities between this view of professional enquiry and the approach to professional learning in the HertsCam Network (introduced in Chapter 2). Individuals are supported by membership of the network made up of colleagues all undertaking development work. The practice and development of non-positional leadership are fostered through participation in Teacher Led Development Work groups, many of which include non-teachers such as librarians and learning support assistants, as well as a step-by-step guide that helps teachers focus and structure their work. In the first five steps, the teacher clarifies their professional values, identifies a concern, negotiates with colleagues to explore that concern, designs and produces an action plan for a development project (a process of change) and negotiates with colleagues to refine the practicality of the project (Hill, 2014). With the sixth and seventh steps, the collaborative process is extended and made more explicit: teachers 'lead projects that draw colleagues, students and their families into collaborative processes' (step 6) and 'contribute to knowledge building in their networks and educational systems' (step 7) (Hill, 2014: 78). Networking is a key facet which enables teachers to improve practice and enhance professional knowledge. Teachers come together at regular network events to take 'our tacit knowledge ... and make it visible' (Anderson et al., 2014: 121). Thus, knowing in practice is shared through socially distributed, action-focused activity. Accounts of teacher-led projects are shared in networking events involving teachers from different schools, leading to insights which others can apply to their own situations.

[T]hey may adopt specific tools or techniques for use in their own practice, but perhaps more importantly they may acquire new ideas, understanding and value positions. In other words, they might gain the 'practical wisdom' which is validated through its impact on classrooms and students' learning. (ibid.)

Through these steps and the collaborative process of enquiry, teachers simultaneously improve practice and develop their teacher leadership.

A final example is that of co-operative professional development in a Co-operative Academy, investigated by Sarah Jones from the perspective of being the school's vice principal. A group of teachers in the school formed the Learning School Improvement Group (LSIG) as an alternative to traditional professional development and with the aim of improving pedagogy and learning. The group is a means by which teachers can initiate change autonomously and has subsequently evolved into multiple LSIGs to allow greater scope for innovation and for teachers to follow up ideas. The LSIGs are guided by co-operative principles and aim for a collegial approach in which colleagues challenge each other's thinking and evaluate practice. The LSIG was set up so that improvements were 'not driven by the "fear factor" of surveillance and judgement but rather by the "peer factor" where teachers held themselves and others accountable' (Jones, 2015: 79). We will return to this example in the next chapter.

Summary

In this chapter we have commended the idea of a learning model of developing collaborative leadership, contrasting this with a transmission model. A learning model is characterised by a journey of discovery that involves people developing through knowing in practice and collaborative enquiry in which knowledge is made visible and shared. Knowing in practice entails questioning and problem-solving, together with the generation of creative responses, applied and evaluated in practice. It involves engaging in self-development – the self-activity that is integral to leadership as learning, discussed in Chapter 6 – and critical reflexivity. Collaborative learning, embedded in a culture of collaborative enquiry and connectivity, is at the core of the model.

The learning model can be seen as the day-to-day operation of leadership as a reciprocal learning process, explored in the previous chapter. All who contribute to leadership are also contributing to the learning of themselves and others through their leadership relationships. The model promotes learning from doing leadership and taking initiatives, and amending ideas and practice in light of this, whilst using published scholarship and research to inform thinking and generate critical questions. Plans are thus provisional and open to feedback, rather than being linear paths to follow. To put it in a nutshell, in the process or journey that the learning model of leadership development represents, leadership awareness and capabilities are developed through leading change.

It is clear that developing leadership in the way indicated by a learning model is not an individualistic matter. Not only is its collaborative nature crucial, the chapter drew attention to examples of supportive structures and guides to action:

collaborative leadership learning groups, the Critical Collaborative Professional Enquiry programme, the HertsCam teacher-led development work groups and related support, and the Learning School Improvement Group approach in a co-operative school. Wenger argues that despite the 'undesignability' of learning, an architecture or framework for learning does need to be designed. This includes a dynamic relationship between what he calls reification and participation. The question is how much of each you have: 'Design for practice is always distributed between participation [freed agency] and reification [enabling structures] – and its realisation depends on how these two sides fit together' (Wenger, 1998: 232). We explore in the next chapter the interaction between structure on the one hand and people's action and reflections on the other, and the creative spaces for learning and the formation of critical intentionalities that are thereby created.

8

Developing Collaborative Leadership: Enabling Structures and Creative Spaces

Introduction

This chapter explores the structures and emergent spaces that facilitate learning and critical intentionality, and hence give sustenance to creativity and the freedom to engage in pro-active agency. The dynamics in these spaces create possibilities for people to formulate intentions and take initiatives, individually and in collaboration with others, and to help shape the leadership that emerges.

Leadership is as much a product of the organisation as the individual. This is another way of saying that leadership is both emergent and intentional. It involves social processes and agency. We use the trialectic view of social dynamics as an analytical frame to help capture this understanding of leadership. The trialectic frame (see Figure 8.1), based on the sociological theory of analytical dualism (Archer, 2003), articulates social processes as an ongoing interaction between structure, person and practice (Woods, 2005, 2016a). Structure has three parts: culture, institutional architecture and the social environment. These parts are discussed further below. The person refers to personal characteristics, such as capabilities, motivations and values. Practice refers to actions taken by

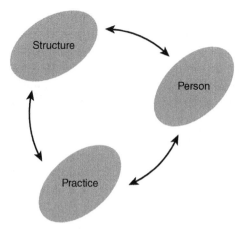

Figure 8.1 Trialectic process
Source: Woods, 2016a: 71

the person with and through other social actors. Within this continuous interaction, structures, persons and practice are shaped by and shape each other.

Some suggest that leadership occurs in the spaces between individuals (Denyer and Turnbull James, 2016: 264). In the trialectic process, the interactions within and between structures, persons and practice imply the idea of spaces within which interactions occur that give rise to intentionalities and the emergence of leadership. We turn to structure first and the importance of enabling structures. We then set out some different kinds of spaces, using the interplay between the parts of the trialectic process as a way of presenting these.

Enabling structures

An implication of a shift to seeing leadership as an emergent and distributed phenomenon is that we should 'aim to shape and nurture contexts where dispersed leadership begins to emerge from all parts of the organisation' (Western, 2013: 317). If interactions and the processes of leadership practice are complex, as complexity theory rightly highlights, how can we move beyond concluding simply that leadership is a messy business that is too confused and tangled to understand and practice better? We can assert that it involves perpetual learning, questioning and problem-solving by participants and the generation of creative responses that are applied and evaluated in practice, as Chapters 6 and 7 have suggested. But can we say more? It is helpful and feasible, we would argue, to throw light on important features that influence complex processes of emergence. In this spirit, we sketch an overview of structures which help to support and facilitate collaborative leadership.

Such enabling structures facilitate organisational actors developing and exercising critically reflexive intentionality and pro-active agency. The discussion draws from the review in Chapter 2 of factors which research suggests are conducive to leadership as a distributed process working effectively. It is also informed by research which suggests that the development of supportive cultures, a collegial climate and institutional changes that facilitate networking, reconfigure team and other group working arrangements and 'interrupt hierarchy', have positive impacts on the leadership capacity of teachers and other non-positional leaders (Drew at al., 2016; Theoharis and Causton, 2014; Woods et al., 2016).

Certain structural factors are conducive to distributed leadership working well (Chapter 2): co-ordination and planning, a cohesive culture, an internal accountability system, resources for capability development, and a committed focus on learning. Of course, how 'working well' is conceptualised – that is, the criteria by which 'wellness' is judged – is crucial to what kind of schooling experience is created. Crucial too is the practical content of these factors. The content of the planning strategy and of the values espoused in the shared culture, for example, will vary according to the philosophy of education, explicit or implicit, informing the day-to-day practice and intentionalities of the school.

Our interest is in the kind of structures that are conducive to, and thus help to enable, collaborative leadership. The value-base for this leadership comprises the values of a philosophy of co-development which can be summarised at its simplest as an imperative to focus attention on improving leadership in two ways: by fostering inclusive participation – so that participation in its practice is open, fair and widespread across those in non-positional roles – and holistic growth. This summary is based on the concept of holistic democracy (Chapter 5), which envisages leadership as a distributed and democratic practice that strives to create opportunities for people to grow as whole persons, able to forge a meaningful life, and to participate in the co-creation of their social and organisational environment, in a climate that promotes mutual respect, critical dialogue, independent thinking and belonging. Integral to holistic democratic practice is an expansive notion of social justice that is concerned to tackle inequalities in learning, participation, respect and resources.

Our proposition is that a structure that is conducive to and helps to enable collaborative leadership conceived in this way combines a participatory culture, an enabling institutional architecture and an open social environment. We now explore each of these in turn.

Here we define culture as the bank of ideas and values that constitute the shared organisational background that people experience and that act as significant guides to priorities and expectations in relation to practice. The culture is a living process of communication and exchange. It includes ideas that are prominently displayed, in reports, on corridor walls, through the organisational website and in other ways, but also discourses that characterise the organisation.

Discourses include not only what senior positional leaders say but also the frequent topics, beliefs and values that people throughout the organisation talk about concerning their roles and practice. The mobilisation of discourse that occurs at national and other policy levels, to create 'coherence and meaning through the promotion of particular narratives' (Arnott and Ozga, 2016: 257), occurs also within organisations like schools.

In a *participatory culture*, the cultural bank values and communicates ideas on leadership as a process involving many different people across the organisation. A participatory culture will tend to give room for discussion of the value of leadership as a distributed practice and to symbolic messages that signal the importance given to respect and social justice. In a school, this includes a culture 'in which school staff members embrace a collective ethos that all students are their students and work together to know and respond to students collaboratively' (Theoharis and Causton, 2014: 97). In so far as conscious efforts are made by those in positional and non-positional roles to give momentum to these kinds of ideas and values, a discourse of collaborative leadership is being mobilised. This helps to contribute as a living part of each day to the firm framing we referred to in Chapter 2 – that is, a clear framework of values, purpose and structures that help to support the development and practice of collaborative leadership.

Jo Mylles (2017), a deputy headteacher, explains how her school's association with the HertsCam Network has enabled the school to develop and sustain a participatory culture. This culture supports both the clear articulation of their approach to school improvement and teacher leadership and the practices which lead to such improvement and enable teacher leadership to be a sustained way of working in the school. In Jo's view, senior leaders need to work to develop cultures which allow teachers' agency and structures which support it. The articulation of ideas and values and active discourses around these is a crucial part of doing this. She recognises the influence of ideas in the leadership literature and refers to the concept of servant leadership which influenced their approach in her school. 'Rituals', as she describes them, are integral to staff briefing every week: these rituals enable colleagues to share knowledge that can be adapted in their practices. (There is more about these rituals below.) This observation by Jo provides an illustration of one way in which a participatory culture is created in this school through mobilising a discourse of participatory and pro-active non-positional leadership:

> The briefings are often filled with laughter and jokes when strategies are shared which *helps us reaffirm our shared purpose and values*. (Mylles, 2017: 109; emphasis added)

Turning to institutional structures, we refer to these as institutional architecture, covering institutional arrangements, such as job descriptions, line management organisation, the membership and functions of committees, meetings and working groups and systems of resource allocation, which allow an organisation to function. *Enabling institutional architecture* facilitates and supports leadership from across all parts of the organisation and the values of inclusive participation and holistic growth. Examples, according to context, could include widening membership of committees, teams and working groups (for example, enabling ad hoc working groups to be set up easily by staff and/or students that bring together different people to work collaboratively on projects bringing about change), allocating financial and/or time resources in ways that support pro-active agency (for example, giving staff and students opportunities to develop capabilities in leadership, collaborative working and innovation), and supporting non-positional teacher, student and other leadership roles. In their research into enabling structures for professional learning communities, Gray et al. (2016: 879) cite opportunities for teachers to meet and collaboratively plan lessons, the development of interdependent teaching roles and regularly scheduled time for professional development.

An example of an innovation in enabling institutional architecture is the form and purpose of Teacher Led Development Work groups. These are part of the HertsCam way of developing teacher leadership and were mentioned in the previous chapter. Teachers are supported in exercising reflexive intentionality and pro-active agency by being members of such groups. Membership helps to sustain them as the type of professional who intends to take a pro-active role in the development of practice, in school improvement and in the building of professional knowledge (Woods et al., 2016).

The rituals that Jo Mylles referred to above are another example of enabling institutional architecture. She writes that, in order to enable dialogue and to make collaboration evident, the school

> developed processes for colleagues ... that are woven into the fabric of the school. We have rituals during staff briefing every Friday to enable members of staff to talk about teaching and learning. A recent theme was 'Foiling Flamel' where each week on a rotation basis a subject based team would heroically save teaching and learning strategies from the villain Flamel and submit them to one of the Assistant Headteachers who would keep them safe. (Mylles, 2017: 109)

Under the discussion of participatory culture, we drew attention to how these rituals helped to communicate ideas and affirm shared values and the purpose of that culture. Here we are highlighting the institutional design of this participative event. It is designed as a forum in which sharing and collaboration can take place. It has a custom of being both work-focused but also being enjoyable – a custom that is likely emergent from the people participating and what then becomes an expectation of how it works (rather than the custom being simply the product of a senior leader). It is weekly and regularly scheduled on a particular day. These are some of the institutional features that give the collaborative event a form and structure.

The social environment refers to the patterns and climate of relationships. This is the third aspect of the structure in the trialectic process. It is another important structural variable in influencing whether collaborative leadership is encouraged, with people enabled to develop a pro-active and critical approach to formulating intentions and taking initiatives, individually and in collaboration with others. We describe the social environment that fosters collaborative leadership as an *open social environment*. It is an environment in which positive relationships across status and other organisational boundaries are readily established to initiate and develop change. A deputy headteacher described one of the benefits of an innovative approach to collaborative innovation in her school: 'it really works for school improvement because you are *working collegiately with staff* who are actually going to be involved in delivering the changes and measuring the impact' (Drew et al., 2016: 101; emphasis added). An open social environment is characterised by stimulating connections and connectivity (Chapter 6). There is a shared, equal social authority amongst organisational members to initiate and be involved in change, even though there may be distinctions in formal authority and other differences between people. There are nurturing affective bonds and values expressed in relationships: belonging, social equality, flexibility, fluidity, openness, respect, trust and mutually affirming relationships are all important in this social environment.

These are the kinds of features important for communities of collaborative leadership practice that are sites and sources of leadership across the school landscape (Chapter 6). A large number and diversity of communities of leadership practice may represent an active and widely participative distribution of leadership. The Learning School Improvement Groups (LSIGs), examined by Sarah Jones (2015) writing as a vice principal of the school in which they have been developed, can be viewed as communities of collaborative leadership practice. (These groups were discussed in Chapter 7.) They aspire to be collegial, drawing on co-operative values.

> Through co-operation we assume that all participants act as autonomous agents and that they will seek to improve their work as well as that of others ... It is possible to draw upon the values of equality and equity to ensure equal participation and solidarity in letting no one fail. The sense of well-being that is unleashed by paying attention to these values is created and nourished by genuine power-sharing and purposeful and transformational dialogue. (Jones, 2015: 77)

Sarah is candid about the tensions and conflicts that arise and that can undermine collegiality and the positive work of these groups: 'all is not rosy in the garden' (Jones, 2015: 80; see also Woods, 2016b). It is useful to be explicit that open social environments will have their tensions and conflicts. Problems that she observed arising include difficulties for new participants in joining existing groups and partnerships, strains between colleagues leading to genuinely heated arguments, tensions between being simultaneously co-operative colleagues and rivals for scarce material rewards, short-termism (a tendency for some teachers to gravitate to groups that could bring about quick gains), loss of momentum at certain times of the year, and some teachers sticking to traditional practices by making only minor changes and presenting them as completely new innovations. Recognising that there are conflicts does not necessarily mean intervention is appropriate. Sarah writes that where there was argument 'I soon discovered that, over time, if left alone, this turmoil and argument has often righted itself and newly co-constructed ideas have developed' (Jones, 2015: 82). Equally important are the ways in which the overarching co-operative ideas (the participatory culture) and institutional arrangements for co-operative practice (the enabling institutional architecture) are designed and able to change as needed. For example, the school started with one large LSIG, but members of this first group concluded after a time that it needed to allow new LSIGs to be started so as to enable new ideas to flourish, one of the reasons being that more experienced LSIG members could inhibit other members. There are rules across the community of LSIGs 'to define the position of members and their activity' (Jones, 2015: 84), but they are not imposed for all time and can be supplemented by individual groups and may be negotiated by new members. There are no guarantees that collegiality will always result. The character of the groups emerges from individuals talking with colleagues and positioning themselves in relation to the firm framing offered by co-operative values.

The point about newcomers experiencing difficulty in breaking into existing groups highlights an important issue for communities of collaborative leadership practice. Such communities are capable of having hard boundaries and identities amongst participants that lead them to be focused inwardly on their own community. Yet, as research on innovation suggests (Chapter 2), new ideas and development of innovative practices are favoured by boundary-crossing. Communities of leadership practice that are too tightly focused inwardly may lessen the connectivity across a school. An open social environment therefore has not only strong group bonds but also ties across boundaries which encourage diversity of thinking and experience. This avoids an organisational landscape of 'tightly connected groups with few connections between the groups' (Seel, 2006: 3) and consequent confinement within a too comfortable state of belonging, either within the school or within its departments, groups and teams.

Creative spaces

Interplays can be seen as occurring in spaces. These spaces are the areas in which interplays take place over time and in which there is, *inter alia*, creativity and compliance, indeterminateness and repeated patterns, protection and risk.

The multiple and varied activities in such spaces are both an aspect of complexity and a reason for it.

We distinguish here between four spaces. These distinctions are helpful analytically as they are an aid to organising thinking about emergence and the changes that occur through complex processes and interactions.

The first space we highlight is the *trialectic space* itself – the whole – which represents the interplay between structure, person and practice. This is the area symbolised by Figure 8.1. Organisational life is given momentum through the animated parts of the trialectic space. People, their relationships and their actions provide the living impulses which create movement, change and stability. Two spaces, or sub-spaces, within the trialectic space can be identified which focus attention on these living impulses.

The first sub-space is *agency space*. We are defining agency as the power of people to think, feel and act, as explained in Chapter 5. This space therefore covers the person and practice, and their interactions, as shown in the larger oval in Figure 8.2. Agency encompasses the doing and the intentionality (reflecting, deliberating, feeling, formulating of will and intentions), as well as the person's capabilities, dispositions and so on, and highlights the interactive processes between these.

The second sub-space analytically represents an aspect of the person. It throws attention on the internal or *subjective space* of the person within the agency space. It is shown by the smaller oval, within the person, in Figure 8.2. This is the personal process of self-activity (Chapter 6), and includes the processes of intentionality. Feelings, willing and cognitive thinking, as well as interactions with other people involving shared discussions and consideration,

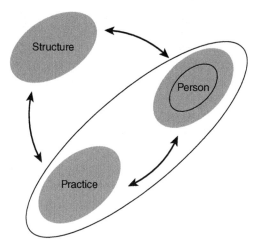

Figure 8.2 Trialectic process showing agency and subjective spaces (based on the figure in Woods, 2016a: 71)

feed into the deliberations in this space. From these processes and interactions intentions and the will to action emerge. In collaborative leadership, pro-active agency is the enactment of change and purposeful innovation underlined by the value-base of holistic democracy and social justice, and such pro-active agency arises from critical intentionality. The latter is characterised by critical reflexivity that is willing to be both self-critical and critically evaluative of practice, asking hard questions that bring to the surface assumptions, limits and blindspots as well as the degree to which practice is achieving planned aims.

Simon Western (2012, 2013) identifies the value of thinking spaces. A coach can create a thinking space to help someone engage their subjective space in a focused and concentrated way. The thinking space is internal – a place 'to stop, to reflect, to muse, to consider, to drift and to contemplate' (Western, 2013: 319). Western's discussion of it illustrates also how support and collaboration – that is, external interactions – are important factors in its development. The activity of the thinking space is internal contemplation and it can be difficult to reach by individuals acting in a world focused on speed, action and competition. Western describes coaching as the catalyst which supports the creation of a space in which individuals can be creative and where critical perspectives are encouraged in order to support the development of a way forward.[1]

There is an interesting link here to Margaret Archer's (2003) proposition of the internal conversation as a way by which individuals increase control over their lives. It is this internal conversation which shapes the relationship between structure and agency as it impacts on individuals in day-to-day living. Coaching provides explicit external support for individuals to exercise their autonomy in deciding both what to aim for and the best courses of action. It is the internal conversation externalised, whilst retaining a focus on the coachee and their agenda.

The dynamic for change is the product of the interactions that occur in and between the spaces we have been discussing. At the core of collaborative leadership is freedom, by which we mean relational freedom in which the person has a significant degree of self-direction as an individual and as a social being and there is mutually supporting growth, amongst the self and others, towards autonomy (Chapter 5). The development of collaborative leadership involves the nurturing of critical reflexivity and pro-active agency which is about initiating change and 'making a difference' (Frost, 2006). Personal intentionality occurs in the internal, personal space – the subjective space – where critical reflexivity is able to grow and be used; but we can see from our discussion of the trialectic and agency spaces how the subjective space is embedded in wider interactions and structures.

---

1 Coaching and mentoring are used a great deal in leadership development though how they are practised and interpreted varies greatly (Bush, 2010: 118–119).

As well as the trialectic, agency and subjective spaces, there are *physical and socially created spaces*. Spaces for reflection, social get-togethers, discussion, exchange and debate are part of the organisational texture of participatory organisational environments that nurture holistic growth and critical reflexivity (Fielding, 2009; Woods, 2005). As an example of designing opportunity for personal reflection, Western (2013: 318) commends the Contemplation Pods built into the architectural design of the Scottish Parliament. Participatory practice in schools benefits from social spaces that allow interactions and shared deliberations without the constraints of hierarchy and the usual boundaries between people – spaces that have been termed 'free spaces' (Woods, 2005: 89–92). Such free spaces include 'independent zones' where groups with little or no formal authority, or marginal and disadvantaged groups, are able to come together, share experiences and ideas, provide mutual support and work together for change. Examples include student-initiated and student-led project groups such as those facilitated in schools by the Learning to Lead approach to student participation (Woods, 2011: 140–142), as well as groups or teams comprising teachers working without senior leadership involvement. Another kind of free space is the 'blurred status arena' where there is scope for informal interactions and exchanges across normal organisational boundaries and where constraints of hierarchical status and authority are minimised. These would be spaces where senior leaders and staff, or teachers and students, mix without hierarchical consciousness (Woods, 2005: 90–92). An example is given in Chapter 6, where a newly qualified teacher facilitates learning amongst more established colleagues by creating spaces for them to engage in self-activity and self-development concerning an innovation the teacher is leading.

Fielding (2009: 498) emphasises the need for these to include open or public spaces where

> staff and students can reflect on and make meaning of their work together and develop shared commitments to further developing the ideals and practices of life and learning to which the school aspires.

The rituals built into the institutional architecture of Jo Mylles's school, which we mentioned earlier in this chapter, are an example of a kind of free space that is deliberately created. Like all free spaces, it is structured but also in its operation free from that external structure, allowing freedom of discussion and relatively informal interaction. The enabling structures discussed in the previous section offer a firm framing that democratic ways of practice require. For example, participatory values in the culture constitute a shared organisational background that people experience and act as significant guides to practice and relationships. However, as noted elsewhere, it is not just the firm framing that is essential. A democratic leadership culture has a bivalent character: it 'requires an organisational dynamic that allows for movement between relatively tight and relatively loose structural frameworks', with the firm framing embracing and protecting looser, flexible spaces (Woods, 2005: 87–88).

What we hope this discussion makes clear is that there is a range of spaces whose dynamics influence whether and in what ways collaborative leadership practice develops. These include the subjective space of the person. These are not automatically spaces for creativity and critical reflexivity; but they can be, or can grow to have this character through personal will and activity (for example, developing a questioning approach, engaging with alternative viewpoints through systematic study) and through relationships and support, whether that be coaching or participation in leadership groups led by teachers or students or others in non-positional roles. The latter groups are examples of another kind of space highlighted – physical and social spaces. Again, these are not automatically creative spaces where collaborative leadership can flourish. But they can be where they are constituted as, or become, free spaces where interactions and shared deliberations take place without the constraints of hierarchy and the usual boundaries between people.

Summary

This chapter has offered an overview of interacting structures and spaces that help to promote collaborative leadership, using the framework of the trialectic view of social dynamics to represent the ongoing interactions between structure, person and practice. The overview, rather than being a blueprint for change, is intended to be a resource to inform collaborative leadership development in a school or other setting.

The chapter set out the kind of structures and their specific characters that are likely to enable such leadership: a participatory culture, enabling institutional architecture and an open social environment. It then identified some of the spaces within which interplays occur between structure, person and practice, and within the person. These include agency space which covers the person and practice, and their interactions, and subjective space. The latter encompasses processes of self-activity and personal intentionality, as well as feelings and cognitive thinking, from which intentions and the will to action emerge. The human mobilisation of change arises from the intentionality that develops in the subjective space, within wider spaces of interaction: it is that human mobilisation – the human sparking of change – that for us is important to recognise through the concept of intentionality alongside that of emergence. Critical intentionality that fosters pro-active agency and exercises critical reflexivity is crucial for collaborative leadership.

It was also recognised that the internal processes of the subjective space occur within and are to some degree shaped by the outer supports available or created.

Such supports include relationships like coaching, as well as enabling structures and free spaces that help to nurture reflection and collaborative interactions. By facilitating critical reflexivity, these play a part in enhancing the freedom and a sense of agency that is at the heart of collaborative leadership.

We now turn in the next chapter to an exploration of the vital importance of non-positional agency, as well as positional, senior-leadership agency, in the active work of developing leadership. That is followed in Chapter 10 by a discussion of identity change through key practices in the development of collaborative leadership.

9

Developing Collaborative Leadership: Change from across the Leadership Landscape

Introduction

In Chapter 4, the challenges posed by complexity theory and understanding leadership as emergent were examined. The question was posed: if senior leaders cannot act as 'godlike' actors seeing the organisation or system from the outside, what is the nature of their role? What is clear is that the role of senior leaders is not expunged by understanding leadership as emergent and that varying degrees of hierarchy and of both directive and distributed leadership are possible (Day et al., 2009; Gronn, 2009). One of the implications is that senior leaders have to find ways of stepping back from their traditional power and authority (Harris, 2012; Woods, 2005). As was apparent from the discussion in Chapter 7, it is not correct to shift from a simple top-down model of leadership to a more sophisticated conception of senior leaders as background manipulators who act by finding and shifting the right levers of change. There we noted the salience of collaborative enquiry as a central part of the learning model of leadership development.

Our interest here is the role of both non-positional and positional leadership in advancing collaborative leadership. We examine this in the context of organisational complexity and everyday processes of authorisation which determine who is being authorised and who is not, and what authorities are seen as having greater or lesser importance. The chapter emphasises that leadership development arises from actions and interactions across the school, with the implication that collaborative leadership must be discursively and collectively created over time by the school's whole leadership population. We close with critical questions on social justice which can be used to aid critical reflexivity concerning the actual operation and development of communities of leadership practice.

Challenges of complexity for developing collaborative leadership

Senior leaders are institutionally designated as 'senior' because of their possession of a specific type of authority – namely (in modern organisations) the formal legal–rational authority of superior posts. By senior leader we are meaning someone with the designated superior authority position in a defined organisational space – such as a head of a school, a department head, a designated group leader, and so on. They are therefore the source of an influential force seeking to co-ordinate the resources, knowledge, and actions of a complex set of agents and relationships. Being aware of leadership as emergent and distributed has implications for the role of senior leaders and how we might understand the power or force that they can exert. Appreciating complexity means that 'rather than seeking closure and certainty, an effective policymaker or school leader would be open to not knowing in advance. He [sic] would respect and encourage local conversations as vital in providing conditions in which novel meanings of educational transformation can be found' (Bates, 2016: 55). This observation commends humility amongst senior leaders.

There are challenges, however, in trying to envisage the role of senior leaders differently and putting into practice the 'stepping back' from traditional, hierarchical leadership that is implied by collaborative leadership. Complexity theory suggests that it is a flaw to see senior leaders as able to stand separate from the organisation and to direct it, as they are embedded in the organisation as a 'living system' (Griffin, 2002: 61). At the same time, however, senior leaders have legitimate authority to mobilise key resources that others within the school do not. This does not mean that they can enact change through a simple process of linear control. However, they can materially affect others and what happens, for good or ill.

Ralph Stacey argues that senior leaders are both subject to discipline (discipline being 'the training of individuals so that they become more economically and socially useful') and 'prime agents' in administering techniques of discipline (2012: 66–67, 70). Such an argument suggests that we should see senior leaders as confined within an economistic and performative view of organisational purpose. They are confined, in this argument, within constraints that necessitate their following narrowly conceived functional aims. Whilst Stacey has a point in recognising that senior leaders are subject to discipline and may feel inclined or forced to yield to this, should we be constrained to see them as always and necessarily so confined?

There are other possibilities. The formal, positional authority of senior leaders may be used with wider and different aims in mind. A headteacher may adopt an 'enabling role' committed to encouraging an 'ethos of a more holistic, child-centred education' (Bates, 2016: 148). David Frost (2011: 12) highlights the crucial role of senior leaders and the importance of the 'deliberate cultivation within the school' of teacher leadership:

> Teachers are unlikely to sustain their capacity for leadership or successfully undertake a development project unless they have active support from their colleagues and in particular from the senior leadership team. There is a growing body of evidence that illuminates the role of senior leaders in facilitating teacher leadership … There are very specific things that principals/headteachers do such as making additional time available or helping to facilitate opportunities for collaboration, but the more fundamental task is concerned with culture building or creating the conditions in which teacher leadership can flourish …

A headteacher in the HertsCam Network explains in what way she sees the senior leaders' role as critical and as scaffolding collective learning (HertsCam Network, 2011: 4):

> The role of the leadership team is pivotal [if we want teachers to build knowledge about teaching and learning together] and we have learned much about how to scaffold this learning from using Inset [in-service professional training] time for teachers to lead the learning of other teachers, to using Inset days to visit other schools using a thinking routine 'Connect, Extend, Challenge' (Perkins), to using niches in the school day for reading groups and learning lunches.

For teachers' collaborative development work to take place and teacher leadership to flourish 'it is important that school principals take positive steps to cultivate professional cultures that are enabling' (Frost, 2011: 43). This is the essential message of notions of leadership such as learning leadership and leadership for learning (Kools and Stoll, 2016; Lingard et al., 2003). Arguably, the defining feature of learning leadership, which Marco Kools and Louise Stoll commend, is its support for the creation of a professional learning community in which the senior leader is a learner. Effective professional learning communities, according to the work of Ray Bolam and colleagues, 'fully exhibit eight key characteristics: shared values and vision; collective responsibility for pupils' learning; collaboration focused on learning; individual and collective professional learning; reflective professional enquiry; openness; networks and partnerships; inclusive membership; mutual trust, respect and support' (Bolam et al., 2005: 145). The ideal community engages in everyday interactions that have the characteristics of the transforming dialogue dimension of holistic democracy. Trust and respect are features that have to be nurtured and achieved through critical questioning about who may be given less respect or trust, either consciously or unconsciously, and why this is. Working to advance cultural justice is therefore a necessary part of developing an environment where there can be transforming dialogue.

In the learning leadership discourse, the senior leader plays the key role in creating a professional learning community – putting learning at the centre, modelling and championing what this means, setting the tone through daily interactions and challenging organisational inhibitors to the creation of such a community (Kools and Stoll, 2016: 58–61). The leadership role in this view focuses mostly on the senior leader deploying their authority to generate a learning-focused environment. However, arguments for such learning leadership do not necessarily incorporate collaborative leadership as conceptualised in this book.

The international Carpe Vitam Leadership for Learning project (see also Chapters 2 and 6) is distinctive in making explicit the importance of infusing a shared leadership culture with democratic values (Frost and Roberts, 2011; Swaffield, 2014). The project concluded through its international work and the data it collected that 'shared leadership' (the project's preferred term) 'is something that principals, teachers and students increasingly aspire to', but it also noted how shared leadership 'is understood quite differently in different settings' (sometimes as delegation) and how 'deeply embedded conceptions of leadership are' (Frost et al., 2008: 5). The latter point highlights the power of the persistence of hierarchical framing of leadership, abetted by the reality of the powerful legitimacy and resources which senior leaders have. It is no surprise then that critical examinations of distributed leadership highlight the power of senior leaders. A study of three primary schools in Scotland, for example, concluded that to a large extent 'distributed leadership was found to be in the gift of the headteacher, actively encouraging, enabling and facilitating distributed leadership at individual and whole staff levels' (Torrance, 2013: 50). The study elaborates:

> Each of the headteachers was articulate, highly reflective on their practice and committed to making sense of a distributed perspective on leadership and management. They had learned hard lessons along the way. They articulated tensions related to their intentions to engage staff, which could be interpreted as knowing how to elicit the best efforts of their staff, 'new managerialist' strategies or even manipulation. (Torrance, 2013: 60)

Should we conclude from this that collaborative leadership is simply a different kind of dependency than traditional hierarchical leadership which remains subject to the ultimate power of senior leaders? We would argue not. Advancing social justice and enabling and sustaining leadership distribution may need determined leadership from the headteacher or senior team, providing 'lead agency' and 'firm framing' (Woods, 2005: 121). However, this is only a part of the picture. Colleen Capper and Michelle Young (2014: 162, 163), for example, refer to 'a combination of superhero/collaborative leadership', but emphasise that 'creating more socially just schools must be understood as the responsibilities of a principal for social justice along with leadership teams and full school communities, rather than the domain of single individuals'.

Authorisation and multiple authorities

A more fundamental shift is needed, beyond a primary focus on the senior leader granting or supporting a collaborative leadership culture or delegating responsibilities. In encouraging this shift, we recognise that there is not one kind of authority but multiple authorities in and across the leadership landscapes within the school. The call to humility on the part of school leaders referred to above is reinforced by recognising that formal hierarchy provides one form of authority, with designated abilities – to deploy organisational resources, for example – amongst a multiplicity of other authorities. The idea of multiple authorities (Woods, 2016b) was introduced in Chapter 6 and some key examples are shown in Figure 9.1, reproducing Figure 6.1. A primary focus on the senior leader granting or supporting a collaborative leadership culture overlooks the plural authorities that can be called on as legitimate bases, not confined to senior leaders, for pro-active agency.

formal	bureaucratic, legal-rational authority in which the holder of a post has authority in a hierarchy of posts
professional expertise	rational authority based on claims to knowledge and capabilities gained through recognised programmes of education and training and command of a body of knowledge
experiential	an acknowledged authoritative character which a person gains through their personal and/or professional history and the responses and actions they have gone through in facing challenges
charismatic	authority accorded to a person because of some special characteristic they have or their force of personality
traditional	authority distributed according to communally legitimised criteria such as gender, ethnicity, age or social class
democratic	authority of a person and the decisions and actions they enact gained through the legitimacy given by an accepted process of participation, dialogue and consent
market	authority for decisions and actions being carried out derived from the legitimacy accorded to the forces of competition and the perceived need to respond to these

Figure 9.1 Types of authority

A senior leader may possess authorities in addition to the formal one, such as outstanding professional expertise or a charismatic presence, but this may not be the case. Crucially, others in a range of non-positional roles may have comparable or even superior expertise in specific aspects of teaching and experience, or carry charismatic or other kinds of authority: they may be seen as possessing professional, experiential or charismatic authorities for example. Multiple authorities may be aligned and operate synergistically in straightforward ways. Equally they may lead to tensions and conflicts.

Recognising the existence of such authorities helps us to understand better the nature, opportunities and challenges of power sharing in collaborative leadership practice. It also leads us to emphasise that an authority is not an objectively owned asset. Instead, it is the ongoing outcome of a relationship between those who are perceived as having authority and those who do the perceiving. As we noted in Chapter 6, it is a process of granting legitimacy by others – a process of authorisation. Equally, it is possible that authorisation may be withheld or reluctantly and less than full-heartedly given. This may affect how far non-positional leaders, such as newly qualified teachers, students or support staff, are given scope to initiate change and be listened to.

The giving or withholding of authorisation affects the degree to which power sharing and transforming dialogue are everyday realities for everyone. Who is being authorised and who not, and what authorities are seen as counting, are key questions in the nurturing and growth of collaborative leadership. A case study of teacher leadership in a US school, for example, found that teachers (female and male) did not accord female teachers professional or experiential authority in disciplinary matters: it was the gender of the male teachers that was perceived as carrying authority (a form of traditional authority in the typology shown in Figure 9.1) (Scribner and Bradley-Levine, 2010).

Leadership development from across the school

This recognition leads us into an argument concerning leadership as reciprocal learning and the integral place of non-positional leadership in this argument. The development of collaborative leadership practice is not simply or even primarily the outcome of senior positional leadership, important though that is. Rather, it is an emergent, ongoing process that relies on leadership being practised as a pedagogical, reciprocal learning process that grows across the school's leadership landscape. If it is to grow and take root, collaborative leadership must be discursively and collectively created over time by the whole leadership population in a school. That population consists of a range of organisational members in non-positional and positional leadership roles, drawing on and co-constructing a range of authorities that they bring and develop. This process of actions and interactions over time fosters a growing identity as leaders, reflecting the general character of collaborative leadership – namely, that leadership emerges from intentionality and agency and the perpetual interactions between people, structures and the environment. Development of collaborative leadership can thus be seen as a pedagogical process, involving reciprocal exchanges across traditional hierarchical boundaries and bringing together different kinds of authority.

There are multiple enactors and creators of leadership. Intentionalities arise at different levels in the organisation: the senior level, at the highest levels of formal authority, being just one level (see Figure 4.1). The wide leadership population, in both non-positional and positional roles, brings diverse experience and expertise – multiple authorities – to processes of reciprocal learning and the initiation of change. It is not a case of someone or some set of senior leaders doing something to another. It is better understood as an organic process in which interconnected parts bring to bear their different and distinctive contributions. Hence, although it is important that 'there should be shared values and vision based on collective responsibility for students' learning ... this [should be] a result of collaborative processes in which all concerned can reflect and engage in enquiry' (Frost, 2011: 43). Evidence from the International Teacher Leadership project suggests that not only does the school principal have a role in culture building (Frost, 2011: 43), but that

> teacher leadership itself plays a major part in helping to create a professional learning community. When teachers take the initiative and lead development projects seen to be beneficial not only to students' learning, but also beneficial in the way they draw colleagues into collaboration and self-evaluation, school principals are able to see significant shifts in the mindset and norms of practice amongst the school staff.

Leadership development, or formation as Western (2013: 311) describes it, requires 'creating spaces, flows and networks that encourage leadership learning and practice'. It is the leadership population of the school, as opposed to just a specific part of this population, such as the senior leadership team, who are engaged in this. By opening opportunities, those less experienced in leadership may develop their leadership at the same time as they contribute their expertise (in a particular area of teaching in which they specialise or are undertaking professional enquiry).

It is worth reinforcing that leadership development is not an individualistic exercise. As emphasised in Chapter 7, the learning model is collaborative; it depends on making operational a culture of collaborative enquiry and connectivity and practising leadership as a reciprocal learning process, through which learning is made visible and is shared and enhanced.

In that chapter, we also suggested that it is useful to view the processes of leadership in a school as occurring across a landscape of leadership practice, made up of numerous communities of leadership practice. We noted how there may be differences between such communities. For example, all will have individual intentionalities, but some may have greater opportunities than others for group-led intentionality with a participatory character, and hence democratic authority underpinning its actions. As networks in which authorisations are formed and take place, they are sites where different authorities are deployed, co-constructed and recognised, or not. A community of practice centred on the senior leadership team possesses a strong degree of formal authority whilst others, such as teacher-led groups, may be more influenced and shaped by professional expertise. However, all will tend to have varying degrees and patterns of charismatic, traditional, democratic and market authority.

A school's landscape of leadership practice is a factor that affects how and where leadership development takes place. The distribution and numbers of communities of leadership practice, the variations and ongoing interactions between them and the multiple authorities that characterise them all have a bearing on leadership development. For example, a small number of active communities of leadership practice concentrated in certain departments of a secondary school, with restricted membership and no actions being taken to extend opportunities will narrow the spread of conscious leadership development as compared with a school where many, diverse communities of leadership practice are the norm and growing.

Critical questions on social justice

We conclude with some questions, offered as an aid to critical reflexivity, relevant to any particular community of leadership practice. Asking who has opportunities and the chance to be included and who has not or is unconsciously overlooked or marginalised is important if the aim of enhancing social justice is a high priority. It provides an opportunity for necessary issues to come to the surface and be responded to. Using the four-fold scheme of social justice (see Figure 5.1), targeted questions can be raised concerning members – and potential members – of a community of leadership practice and how that community works. Questions (a) and (b) are especially relevant to the power sharing and transforming dialogue dimensions of holistic democracy (see the box headed 'Participative dimensions of holistic democracy' in the section on Holistic Democracy, Chapter 5), and question (d) to the holistic learning dimension (see the box headed 'Meaning dimensions of holistic democracy' in the section on Holistic Democracy, Chapter 5); unfairness in relation to question

(c) on resources may have consequences for the practice of any of the holistic democracy dimensions. With regard to a community of leadership practice, which may be a group, department or for the purpose of this exercise the whole school:

a) Does it work in a fair way in enabling participation – in the distribution of opportunities and support to have a voice and contribute to decisions?

b) Does it work in a fair way in encouraging respect and recognition of cultural differences?

c) Does it work to tackle unfairness in resource differences, to reduce unjustified socio-economic inequalities and their negative effects?

d) Does it work in a fair way in enabling learning – in the distribution of opportunities and support for holistic growth?

Addressing such questions is valuable for awareness-raising that feeds into critical intentionalities which in turn influence priorities for change. As Jacky Lumby and Marianne Coleman (2016: 183) argue, 'consistent, persistent action' over the long term is needed to tackle inequalities.

Summary

This chapter has discussed some of the challenges in the role of senior, positional leaders in the complexity that characterises organisations and in seeking to develop collaborative leadership. We argued that the response should not be to concentrate overwhelmingly on senior leadership, but to make a fundamental shift beyond sustaining a primary focus on the senior leader granting or supporting a collaborative leadership culture. Underpinning this shift is the fact that there is not one kind of authority but multiple authorities in and across the leadership landscape within the school. We argued that the focus should be on leadership as a pedagogical, reciprocal learning process which involves actions and interactions by a range of organisational members in non-positional and positional leadership roles across a school leadership landscape. The leadership of those in non-positional leadership positions plays a vital part in helping to create active communities of collaborative leadership practice.

The leadership population in this landscape can draw upon and offer a range of multiple authorities. Authority is not an objective asset, however. It is a legitimacy that is given through an ongoing process of authorising in which everyone across the leadership landscape engages. Authorising may be withheld or given less than wholeheartedly. Processes of authorisation therefore affect who is empowered to enact leadership and who is not and the degree to which power sharing and transforming dialogue are everyday realities for everyone. Leadership distribution has to be accompanied by continual questioning and action about who is being authorised and who is not, and what authorities are seen as counting. Questions were suggested as an aid to critical reflexivity concerning the development and practice of communities of collaborative leadership practice.

10

DEVELOPING COLLABORATIVE LEADERSHIP: IDENTITY CHANGE

Chapter structure

- Introduction
- Clarifying values
- Reframing leadership
- Nurturing key capabilities
- Collective identity construction
- Critical questions on holistic democracy
- Summary

Introduction

Being part of collaborative leadership practice involves changes in how those in both non-positional and positional leadership roles see themselves and the kinds of attitudes and capabilities they see as important for them to foster and develop. As a consequence, these changes have an impact on identity. They are part of creating or evolving a leadership identity. It is important then to consider what we mean by identity.

In everyday parlance, the term 'identity' is used to refer to particular characteristics and attributes of an individual by which we distinguish one person from another – the human capacity to know who is who (Jenkins, 1996). A dominant feature of this way of seeing identity is that it is fixed and inflexible. We know who we are, we know what sort of person another is. We do not expect either us or them to change. The narrowness of this view is exposed through Erikson's (1975) work on identity crisis. Erikson makes a compelling argument for identity as a work in progress, not a fixed state but a process of development. At any given point in time then, we are not so much someone as we are between being one kind of someone, on our way to being the next kind of someone. The 'kind of person we are' can develop from one moment to another as we move between situations and contexts. Brubaker and Cooper's (2000) proposal of the active term 'identification' is a helpful reminder of the danger of assuming that identity is a passive characteristic; it builds on this conceptualisation of identity as activity. It allows us to ask the questions, how do we identify ourselves? How do others identify us? An interesting continuum may be discerned in the literature as authors propose answers to this question. At one end, writers such as Goffman (1959) suggest identity is formed through the self-conscious pursuit of individual interests, with identification with a group emerging as a by-product, whilst Tajfel (1982) represents the opposing view with his proposition of social identity as formed through identification with a group. This view of identity as a meaningful story of the self and relationships is helpful here, allowing us to understand identity as the conduit between structure and spaces, connecting the social and the personal.

Brigid Carroll's (2016) approach to leadership and identity from a practice perspective understands identity as an active process. She views identity as a phenomenon that emerges from contexts and interactions in which people find opportunities for doing leadership, either singly or with others. Leadership identity, from this perspective, concerns the ways in which people 'create and adapt leadership identity through how they use and move through organizational spaces; what routines they build, take part [in] (or not), and disrupt; and how they respond and react to the choices others are making' (2016: 107).

We also highlight the importance of values in constituting identity. The values that 'hold meaning' for individuals, and how these held values relate to each other, significantly shape personal identity (Hitlin, 2003: 123). Values express 'what is important to people' and act as 'guiding principles in people's lives', and hence are central to their concept of self (Schwartz, 2016: 63).

In this chapter, we highlight four practices that we propose are integral to leadership development for collaborative leadership and are constituent elements of ongoing processes of 'identification'. That is, they affect how people understand and feel themselves as active agents in collaborative leadership. All the persons in the trialectic process (see Chapter 8) are animating drivers and influencers of leadership development in a school's landscape of leadership practice. That landscape includes people in both non-positional and positional roles as the previous chapter emphasised. The four practices are relevant to everyone involved in non-positional and positional leadership.

The first two practices are clarifying values and reframing thinking about leadership. We have chosen to consider these because values clarification and reframing thinking about leadership are essential starting points in the long process of changing leadership culture in a school through active and conscious personal involvement across the landscape of leadership practice. This does not mean that values clarification and reframing leadership are once-and-for-all activities; what we are suggesting is that they are essential undertakings at the beginning of change.

The third practice is the nurturing of capabilities. Such nurturing is an ongoing imperative as the distribution of the capabilities across the school's leadership landscape is an important factor affecting the success of collaborative leadership practice. The fourth practice – also an ongoing process – is collective identity construction. We particularly focus on the support and growth that come from this as a shared practice in communities of leadership practice.

Further reflecting the importance of values for identity, in the final section of this chapter, questions framed by the values of holistic democracy are offered as a support to critical reflexivity.

Clarifying values

The philosophy of co-development is a value-base that we consider integral to leadership as a distributed and democratic practice. However, it would be counter to the spirit of this philosophy and the learning model of leadership development to insist that this value-base simply be accepted, or that it be imposed. A founding step for change and developing collaborative leadership is to undertake a process of values clarification. By this we mean, a process in which a teacher (for example) considers what is important to them, what their perceptions of their own priorities are and what they want to make a difference to (Frost and Roberts, 2009).

Experience within the HertsCam Network has shown that the experience of participating in a workshop which enables such a process of values clarification is often a profound experience for participants. Participants are asked to review what they believe in professionally and why. This clarification can take place individually or through colleagues working in pairs to ask and respond to a series of provocations for reflection. Participants frequently comment that it is very unusual to be asked what really matters to them. To be given a space to reflect on their values and to articulate them has a powerful effect on their self-efficacy. It acts as a confirmation of participants' agency and the freedom to focus on the development of an aspect of practice which they feel passionate about (Woods et al., 2016). On a more practical level, it enables them to determine a focus for their development work which is then developed through a strategic plan.

Venetia Norton-Taylor and Sarah Lightfoot (2017), in an account of their teacher-led development work, give a clear insight into the importance of this values clarification process. They explain how their commitment to listening to children and to recognising and respecting their interests directly led to the design of a project which used an innovative pedagogy to support young children in developing their ideas and representing them in creative forms.

Reframing leadership

The power of framing – the tendency to carry round familiar frames of meaning – was alluded to in Chapter 3 in trying to understand the persistence of ideas of hierarchical and 'heroic' leadership. David Denyer and Kim Turnbull James (2016: 264) in their analysis of leadership development observe that every organisation has 'embedded unconscious assumptions about leadership' which constitute a shared 'leadership concept': they conclude that those seeking to develop their leadership need to engage in 'critical reflection to review and/or renew their shared leadership concept'. They draw attention to the philosophical enquiry on leadership by Donna Ladkin who shows the importance – indeed the necessity – of exploring what kind of phenomenon leadership is, in order to 'provide clues about where we might find it and ... where we might most usefully look for it' (Ladkin, 2010: 16). Our articulation of leadership as a phenomenon characterised by intentionality and emergence locates it as a process that emerges from people's intentions and wills and the complex and perpetual interactions that occur across organisations and communities. It is very different from the more traditional concept of hierarchical leadership discussed in Chapter 1.

As with attempts to work out the implications and lessons of complexity theory, a fundamental challenge in developing collaborative leadership is to change mindsets (Boulton et al., 2015: 213). Such development requires a further foundational step, building on values clarification, of reframing leadership. Both these foundational steps give practical expression to practice that nurtures learning and critical reflexivity. They are preparation for leadership practice that continues on these lines – encouraging the self not to accept or seek in others coercive persuasion (see Chapter 6) but to foster reciprocal learning and critical reflexivity.

Reframing has to address both the cognitive and affective dimensions of the frames of meaning through which people navigate the world in their everyday interactions. Cornelissen and Werner (2014) define the cognitive frame as a 'knowledge structure that directs and guides information processing' (2014: 184). The ideas through which we see and interpret the world constitute the cognitive frame.

Affective and emotional responses and associations are, however, integral to understanding frames and their effects. Educational leaders and teachers' emotions are a fundamental aspect of daily practice (Berkovich and Eyal, 2015). Feelings such as those of security, tradition and comfort may reinforce the top-down leadership approach, as well as fear or dislike of alternatives. Moreover, these may not necessarily be overcome simply by the negative feelings that some may associate with hierarchical leadership. Merlijn van Hulst and Dvora Yanow (2016: 105) observe:

> Before one can get to the work of deconstructing and reconstructing frames, emotional issues arising from challenges to personal identities may need to be overcome. Indeed, as Schön argued about social systems ... actors might well fight to remain the same because proposed changes to their definitions of the situation – their framing of it – pose challenges to what they find meaningful, including their sense of self ...

An important process in leadership development, then, is to engage those who are developing their leadership in reflecting critically on the feelings and associations that tend to lead to certain assumptions about leadership. This is as much, or probably more, about affective or emotional reframing as cognitive reframing, since how people feel is so powerful in influencing day-to-day practice. Research in schools, for example, suggests that positive emotional reframing in teachers is associated with strengthening their identity through increasing their perception of occupational self-esteem, motivation, and social acceptance at work (Berkovich and Eyal, 2017). In summary then, rethinking leadership so people can be open to its development as a collaborative practice entails cognitive reframing (how you think) and emotional reframing (how you feel), as well as behavioural reframing (how you act) (Eddolls, 2014: 47).

Nurturing key capabilities

The importance of nurturing leadership capabilities was recognised in Chapter 2, where we also emphasised that fostering leadership capabilities is an ongoing process that includes both support and activity (experiential learning) by all who contribute to leadership, whether through non-positional roles (teachers, students, parents and others) or positional roles (formal leaders). To achieve shared leadership 'requires a conspicuous, planned and systematic investment in relational skills' (Bolden et al., 2015: 2). Moreover, if leadership – as complexity theory and leadership viewed as an emergent process suggest – is not reducible to the learning of certain techniques, procedures and generalisations about effective leading, the capabilities required are more demanding and more ambitious.

We are using the term 'capabilities' here to denote capacities for awareness and learning, skills, behaviours and attitudes that the person draws upon and applies creatively. We suggest such capabilities are resources within the process of exercising the kind of practical judgement that Stacey (2012: 108) commends to deal with 'uncertainty, unpredictability, ambiguity and complexity':

The exercise of practical judgement calls for a wider awareness of the group, organizational and societal patterns within which some issue of importance is being dealt with. This requires a sensitive awareness of more than the focal points in a situation, namely, awareness of what is going on at the margins of what is being taken as the focus. Practical judgement is the experience-based ability to notice more of what is going on and intuit what is most important about a situation. It is the ability to cope with ambiguity and uncertainty, as well as the anxiety this generates.

Whilst written with senior management in mind, the breadth of vision and intuitive ability to spot patterns and identify what is most significant in what is happening has relevance to all who act as leaders or co-leaders.

The practical judgement that Stacey highlights requires to be complemented, as we have indicated, by attending to a range of particular capabilities. This list offers a brief overview of some of the most important.[1]

- **capacity for pro-active agency**, which includes independent thinking, critical reflexivity, clarity of values, confidence and a creative and problem-solving mindset

- **status adaptability**, being able to shed or take status as appropriate, which includes recognising, working with and negotiating multiple authorities as discussed in Chapter 9

- **communicative virtues** which help enable constructive and open exchange – for example being honest and transparent, tolerant, patient, self-controlled, as clear as possible in communications, prepared to express a view, and willing to take criticism and re-examine one's ideas and assumptions; as well as developing abilities to listen, ask questions and respond with feedback in discussions and meetings

- **relational capabilities**, which include skills in developing and sustaining community, working collaboratively and facilitating collaborative work and conflict handling, as well as a predisposition to co-operative working and a sense of co-responsibility; we would include kindness and compassion in this

- **abilities for reciprocal leadership learning**, being able to support others in nurturing their leadership and to share one's own learning and experience of leadership in supportive ways, and to learn from and be supported by others

Collective identity construction

In her investigation of co-operative professional development groups, Sarah Jones emphasises the significance of identity: 'it is through the act of *participation* that identity is constructed: it is not what you know but who you are and

---

1 These are informed by a range of studies which include Bolden et al. (2015: 29–36), Harris and Lambert (2003: 31–32), Klar et al. (2016: 15–16), Ulhøi and Müller (2014: 80) and Woods (2005: Chapter 9 and 2011: 102–106), as well as experience in supporting the development of teacher leadership.

what you become in the practice' (Jones, 2015: 83; original emphasis). Whilst we believe that 'what you know' influences identity change, particularly in the sense of new capabilities a person comes to find important to their intentions and future development, we concur that the experience of collaboration and leading change is a highly significant part of identification.

The aspect that we concentrate on in this section is collective construction of identity in community, which helps to promote collegiality and relational well-being. We do not deny the tensions and conflicts that also occur in identity change, but we focus here on the positives. In the activities of the HertsCam Network collective construction of identity is apparent. The detailed accounts of practical collaboration in Woods et al. (2016: 44) show how teachers can build their identity as teachers who exercise leadership. In relation to the HertsCam way of working, we note too the importance of the construction by teachers of stories or narratives of the change they are making through their development projects. Wenger argues that there 'is a profound connection between identity and practice ... practice entails the negotiation of ways of being a person in that context' (Wenger, 1998: 149). Identity is shaped by and through narratives about practice and their creation – stories of practice. These include both personal stories elaborated in the person's subjective space and shared stories conveyed and co-constructed in interactions between people's agency spaces. Stories may also become part of the structure by, for example, becoming part of the fund of ideas in a shared culture.

This vignette about the HertsCam Annual Conference of teachers and schools in the network gives insight into one of the ways through which a collaborative leadership identity may be nurtured and grown over time.

The conference is an expression and reinforcement of participative identity and active, confident professionalism. This is articulated by one of the key speeches of the 2015 conference, by an assistant headteacher of a HertsCam school and one of the leading co-ordinators of the network.

> ... you keep bringing such passion and energy to HertsCam and it grows because you grow. Each innovation, each collaboration, each tweak to practice shifts the juggernaut and builds our collective professional knowledge, our understanding and probably most importantly our confidence ... We are sometimes guilty of thinking that our work doesn't make a difference in the great scheme of things, that we are too small to be noticed but events like today remind us we are part of something much bigger: we are the grains of sand in a dune that as a single force has the power to cover pyramids. (Speech by Val Hill, in Frost, 2016: 5)

Val Hill goes on to articulate in her speech the essential identity of HertsCam teachers by explaining what HertsCam stands for.

> ... it stands for the power of the individual teacher and our inherent ability to change our part of the world for the better. You begin with your own professional concern and you tackle it, head on, for the benefit of your students and your school. Which sounds as though it could be limited and parochial, doesn't it? And it might well be if it wasn't for the inclusion alongside all that of a gentle but relentless pressure to develop our sense of agency: that powerful drive we all have to be in the driving seat in our lives, whether at home, in the bank or in our workplace. (Speech by Val Hill, in Frost, 2016: 5)

The identity of the teacher as a pro-active agent of positive change – 'the power of the individual teacher' that Val Hill gives prominence to in the speech above – is not a call to individualistic agency, but is made part of a collaborative and collective endeavour. The point is made a key one for the conference – that by 'collaborating and consulting with others we create and share professional knowledge which transforms our work and embeds it into the school culture ...' (speech by Val Hill, in Frost, 2016: 5). The annual conference is a component in the ability of the network to create a sense of belonging. The 2011 evaluation of the network found that this was an important impact.

Belonging to a professional community is important to a lot of teachers and having the opportunity to meet and share with 'like minded' people is a common benefit as described by one teacher following a network event.

> Absolutely invaluable to share ideas and discussion with other teachers. Sometimes schools can be fairly insular places therefore it is motivating and stimulating to hear that others are facing barriers and trying to find solutions. ... Good to link with others as I personally feel working as a partnership is so important to towns such as Stevenage – collaborative work can work so well if it has the foundations to work upon. (Network Evaluation F, 2011, quoted in Wearing, 2011: 44)

The point of significance with regard to this case study is that the conference acts as a collective construction of identity, both by what is said and through the practice of the conference itself. It is an active ingredient in building a culture of collaborative learning that embeds and supports distributed leadership.

(The vignette is an excerpt from Woods et al., 2016: 43–45.)

Critical questions on holistic democracy

Starting explicitly with values clarification, all of the practices discussed in this chapter encourage engagement with questions of values and priorities. To the extent that they are guided by our conception of collaborative leadership, the practices encourage reflection on what aspiring to the values of holistic democracy and social justice mean in any particular school and context. The fundamental concern is how far the actual practices of collaborative leadership are helping to foster relational freedom and mutual supportive growth towards self-awareness and self-determination across the leadership landscape. Questions based on the social justice scheme were offered at the end of Chapter 9. Here, questions based on the dimensions of holistic democracy (Chapter 5) are offered as a further support to critical reflexivity. Reflecting on the practice of collaborative leadership in a school, departmental or other setting,

a)   In what ways is it helping to foster holistic learning?

b)   In what ways is it helping relational well-being?

c)   How successful is it in power sharing?

d)   How successful is it in creating opportunities for transforming dialogue?

Summary

In this chapter we have discussed four practices integral to leadership development for collaborative leadership. These affect how people see and feel themselves as active agents of change and the kinds of attitudes and capabilities they view as important for them to foster and develop. Hence, they have implications for identity and how it changes over time.

Clarifying values and reframing thinking about leadership were the first two practices discussed. These are essential starting points in the long process of changing leadership culture in a school. The continuous imperative to nurture, across the school's leadership landscape, capabilities for collaborative leadership was the third practice outlined. Collective identity construction was the fourth discussed, focusing on this as an ongoing process of shared support and growth in communities of leadership practice. These practices encourage engagement with questions of values and priorities. The chapter concluded with questions based on the dimensions of holistic democracy, offered as a support to critical reflexivity.

The final chapter, to which we now turn, outlines a series of three catalysts for reflection and action, based on key ideas presented in the book.

11

CATALYSTS FOR CHANGE

Chapter structure

- Introduction
- Interconnection of key ideas
- Catalysts for reflection and action
- Summary

Introduction

At the outset of this book we placed freedom at its heart. We started from the position that freedom is an essential part and goal of educational leadership. The book has sought to explain how educators and learners can act with autonomy and play an active part in leadership as an emergent process arising out of people's everyday actions and interactions. In this chapter we draw together key ideas presented in the book and use them as a basis for three catalysts for reflection and action.

Interconnection of key ideas

The book's central focus has been relational freedom – freedom with others. Self-awareness and critical reflexivity are essential constituents of individuals exercising self-direction as social beings. Relational freedom entails both developing in the self and supporting in others growth towards autonomy, as well as responsibility that reflects a deep relatedness to other people, the natural world and those experiences and elements of life, from music to expressions of community, that feed the human spirit (Woods, 2017a). In our view then, a fundamental purpose of an educational system, and of collaborative leadership, is to foster the capabilities and practice that nurture relational freedom amongst those in non-positional and positional roles.

Our conception of collaborative leadership brings together claims about what leadership is and what it ought to be. The basic nature of leadership is the same whether the motives and leadership relationships are authoritarian or demo-cratic. Leadership arises through numerous intentionalities and through emergence. Intentionality is the will or intention to make a difference, with and through others, which leads to action and arises from people as agents express-ing meaning, purpose and goals. Emergence is the perpetual process of complex interactions, involving the interplay of people's intentionalities, actions, ideas, social structures, artefacts, environmental conditions and relationships; out of such interactions come the influences and energies that constitute leadership and give direction to groups and organisations. Intentionalities (from purposive individuals) and emergence (arising from complex interactions) occur simulta-neously and are intertwined.

This first proposition (Chapter 4), concerning what leadership is, can be shaped by and give expression to different values. Leadership may serve to sus-tain the assumptions of a philosophy of dependence – that people are fundamentally dependent on being directed and provided with instructions and definitive guidance in order to know what to do in order to think, feel and behave as good people (Woods, 2016a). This tends to be associated with strongly hierarchical leadership and reliance on 'heroic', controlling or transformational leaders. But, as was made evident in Chapter 3, leadership distribution which blurs or reduces hierarchy may also serve to advance uncritical acceptance of dominant discourses and priorities. Leadership distribution may be deployed in ways and in a context that fosters dependence and discouragement of critical reflexivity.

The value-base of leadership practice has to be explicit and indicate the view taken on what is most important for human flourishing. We contrast the values and beliefs of a philosophy of dependence with those of a philosophy of co-development, and argue that collaborative leadership is founded in a commit-ment to the latter (see Chapter 5). The philosophy of co-development is the view that people are fundamentally capable of growing ethically, intellectually and in other ways through their own actions (their inner and outer practice). Progress in this is not made individualistically but with and by helping others, and people need to be not dependents but co-creators of the social and ideas environments in which they live. This viewpoint is articulated in the ideas and values of holistic democracy. The practice of holistic democracy consists in the opportunity for people to grow as whole persons, able to forge a meaningful life, and to participate in the co-creation of their social and organisational environment, in a climate that promotes mutual respect, critical dialogue, independent thinking and belonging.

The core purpose of holistic democracy is, then, to enable people to develop a capacity for freedom as social beings. It focuses attention on efforts to improve leadership in two areas. The first is inclusive participation, so the voices of all are heard and valued and dialogue is open, respects differences and seeks to learn from others and to find constructive ways of tackling challenges. The second area is holistic growth, which anchors leadership distribution in a framework of deep and holistic learning. Emphasising a concern with fairness and unjustified inequalities, our explanation of the philosophy of co-development includes an expansive view of social justice.

Figure 11.1 is a neater version of the messy diagram in Chapter 5 (see Figure 5.2). It shows leadership being necessarily characterised by intentionality and emergence (our first proposition), but being underpinned by a value-base which may be aligned with very different ideals and assumptions about people. That is, leadership may in its practice be guided more by values associated with dependence or by values associated with co-development. Our second proposition takes a values position and commends a philosophy of co-development as a value-base.

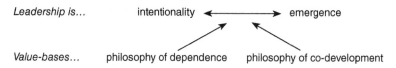

Figure 11.1 Intentionality, emergence and alternative value-bases

We argue that our conceptualisation of collaborative leadership helps in addressing the critiques of distributed leadership examined in Chapter 3: in particular, the difficulties of conceptualising the concept and the criticism that the practice and investigation of distributed leadership too often avoid critical issues of profound importance, in particular social justice, power and inequalities. Collaborative leadership, as we have depicted it, builds in an ethical commitment to a specific value-base. This specificity provides a framework for critical reflection on leadership practice and helps to foster the critical intentionality that is an essential part of relational freedom.

Collaborative leadership has profound implications for the development and practice of leadership. It involves shifts in identity and an active process of identification as a critical and pro-active agent of change. Practices integral to leadership development for collaborative leadership were discussed in the previous chapter. Values clarification and reframing leadership were suggested as essential starting points, for those in non-positional and positional roles, in the long process of changing leadership culture.

Catalysts for reflection and action

In this section we offer sets of questions that can be used or adapted by individuals, teams or a whole school as catalysts for reflection and action planning. They are designed for those in non-positional and positional roles. At the core of the learning model approach (see Chapter 7) is a culture of collaborative enquiry and connectivity through which learning is made visible and is shared and enhanced. The presentation of these questions as catalysts is designed to be used in the spirit of this learning model and to be helpful to those who are engaged in developing collaborative leadership. The structure and content of the questions grow from the argument of the book and are informed particularly by the concept of holistic democracy (see Chapter 5) and the discussion of identity change (see Chapter 10).

These catalysts can be used individually, to support one's own reflections, or addressed collectively, as a team or group to compare understandings, or as a whole school to support leadership development and distribution.

Catalyst 1 – values clarification

Underpinning the thinking behind this catalyst are key ideas introduced in earlier chapters, namely relational freedom, critical intentionality characterised by critical reflexivity, pro-active agency, and the importance of being clear about the value-base of leadership practice. The series of questions in the box below can be used to clarify the values which underpin leadership beliefs and activity.

If a group is going to consider these questions, it may be helpful for the group to read selected parts of the book. We would suggest Chapter 5 (the sections on the need to elaborate values, holistic democracy and social justice) and Chapter 10 (the section on clarifying values).

- What ideas and ethical aims are most important to you?
- What ideas and ethical aims are most evident in your practice?
- In what ways is the context and practice in which you work out of kilter with your values?
- What do you want to be free to do that you are not free to do?
- What would help you to be free?

Catalyst 2 – leadership re-framing

In this book we have presented an argument for leadership as a distributed, emergent idea and practice which is the province of people in both non-positional and positional roles. You may choose to use the questions in the box below to review understandings and practice of leadership in your setting.

If a group is going to consider these questions, it may be helpful for the group to read selected parts of the book. We would suggest Chapter 3 (the section on the persistence of the 'heroic' model), Chapter 4 and Chapter 10 (the section on reframing leadership).

In your setting:

- What do you think leadership is?

- Who should contribute to leadership?

- Who does contribute to leadership?

- Who does not contribute to leadership?

- Who is listened to?

- Who is not listened to?

- What would the first step be if you wanted to distribute leadership more fully?

Catalyst 3 – formulating change to develop collaborative leadership

In this catalyst, school leadership guided by the beliefs and values of a philosophy of dependence is contrasted with school leadership guided by a philosophy of co-development (see Figure 11.2). The catalyst is a development of a 'degrees of democracy framework' based on research concerning holistic democracy and democratic leadership (Woods, 2011; Woods and Woods [G.J.], 2012), which has also been deployed as an analytical framework in US research (Bradley-Levine and Mosier, 2017; Woods, 2017b). The use and impact of the framework in leadership development sessions was reviewed in Woods (G.J.) and Woods (2013).

The descriptions on the right-hand side of Figure 11.2 reflect the dimensions of holistic democracy – holistic learning, relational well-being, power sharing and transforming dialogue. The concept of holistic democracy has been discussed in previous chapters and informed the conception of collaborative leadership set out in the book.

The descriptions on the left-hand side of the catalyst, under the heading of 'dependence', represent practices which foster dependence. For the purpose of presenting the contrast with 'co-development', some of the priorities associated with performative policies towards education have also been included. By performative we mean the view of education that defines it predominantly in terms of narrow, measurable and economistic criteria and success according to standardised tests, often grounded in a 'common-sense' view that competition and using the superiority of the market as a mode of governance (neo-liberalism) are the best ways of organising society (Frost and Roberts, 2011; Ward et al., 2015, 2016). Our argument is that performative priorities tend to reduce learning to the demonstration of ideas, emotions and behaviours that serve measurements, institutional comparisons and the perceived requirements of the economy. They measure people – students and educators – according to these functional criteria, and hence the value of students and educators is dependent on their meeting these measures – rather than in unfolding their potential as persons in the more holistic sense articulated by holistic democracy.

The descriptions under 'dependence' represent a school where there is a strict hierarchy and a directive, top-down practice of leadership; student and professional leadership learning is overwhelmingly defined as success in standardised measures of performance and accumulation of competencies; communication and discussion are predominantly concentrated on telling people what to do and collecting data and other feedback on performance; and relationships are functional with a culture of dependence on authority for direction and reinforcement. Although this paints an extreme and negative picture, this should not be taken to mean that all these features at all times and in all contexts are detrimental. The local context and its guiding aims are crucial. For example, hierarchical leadership can be beneficial depending on how it is practised and the circumstances; gaining skills can advance people's capabilities (in leadership and other practices) and in itself is not an indicator of domination by performative priorities: skills and tests may be embedded and part of wider learning and experience in the kind of participatory culture described in Chapter 8 for example.

The picture painted under 'dependence' is thus intended to be an ideal-typical representation that emphasises certain features and omits others that are part of school life. In this way it heightens the contrast with a leadership culture that aspires to 'co-development'.

This catalyst can be used in a number of ways to support reflection on and support or evaluate changes in leadership beliefs and practice. For example, you may wish to use Figure 11.2 to:

Support individual reflections on the position of your school and its leadership:

- Where is it now?
- Where would you like it to be?
- What changes can you make to move it and your leadership practice towards where you would like it to be?

Support a team exercise in developing the school leadership culture:

- Each team member might highlight in one colour the statements on the catalyst which most closely fit the current picture of the school.

- They might then highlight in another colour the statements they would aspire to.

- The team may then compare responses and, if appropriate, draw up an action plan to move collaboratively from the current to the desired state.

Support a whole-school exercise in developing a school leadership portrait to help annual development planning, guided by these questions:

- Where is the school leadership culture now?

- Where would the school like it to be?

- What are the priorities for change in order to move it towards where the school would like it to be?

If a collective exercise is going to be undertaken to consider these questions, it may be helpful for the group to read selected parts of the book. We would suggest Chapters 4 and 5.

Summary

In this chapter we drew together key ideas presented in this book so as to set up three catalysts for reflection and action. The catalysts were explained and presented as sets of questions that can be used or adapted, by individuals, teams or a whole school, as a means of stimulating reflection and action planning for the development of collaborative leadership. The third catalyst included a figure that facilitates comparison between school leadership guided by the beliefs and values of a philosophy of dependence and school leadership guided by a philosophy of co-development. This does not assume a simple choice can be made between two binary options. The purpose of this comparative catalyst is to facilitate critical reflection on how leadership is practised presently and how it may be changed in ways that free people's energies to co-create education for holistic learning.

Everyone knowingly or unknowingly makes some impact on leadership through its complex emergence in a school. The essence of collaborative

Dependence	Co-development
Instrumental learning	**Holistic learning**
The school values and seeks through its practices to foster student and professional learning that is overwhelmingly defined as being successful in standardised measures of performance and accumulation of competencies.	The school values and seeks through its practices to foster holistic growth in everyone (students and adults), which means developing all human capabilities (spiritual, cognitive, aesthetic, affective, ethical, physical) through collaborative learning.
Functional relationships	**Relational well-being**
The school is characterised predominantly by relationships that are functional; there is very little sense of belonging or common spirit of shared endeavour; and a culture of dependence on authority for direction and reinforcement dominates.	The school has a sense of belonging and community that fosters – people feeling empowered – high self-esteem as a member of the school community – the capacity to think for oneself – a deep sense of connection to other people, the natural world and those things that feed the human spirit.
Power concentration	**Power sharing**
The school has a strict hierarchy and a directive, top-down practice of leadership which means that opportunities to have a say in decisions and to take initiatives are narrowly concentrated at the top of the hierarchy.	Everyone has a say in school decisions that affect them and help shape the aims, values and everyday life of the school; leadership is shared so that everyone is able to exercise leadership themselves and with others by taking initiatives and expressing their identity within the parameters of agreed values and responsibilities.
Linear communication	**Transforming dialogue**
Transmission of ideas, information and instructions is predominantly linear, with little or no exploration of ideas or dialogue to enhance mutual understanding; communication is concentrated on telling people what to do and collecting data and other feedback on performance.	Everyone is able to exchange and explore views with each other and engage in open debate to enhance mutual understanding; dialogue in the school is overwhelmingly characterised by mutual respect, openness to listening to others' viewpoints and the sharing of constructive critique.

Figure 11.2 A catalyst for reflection and formulating change to develop collaborative leadership

leadership is to spread awareness of this, to make it fair and feasible for those in non-positional and positional roles to be a pro-active part of collaborative change, and to build into leadership practice critical reflection on how well holistic learning and social justice are being advanced through that practice.

Collaborative leadership is the everyday practice of nurturing freedom that is meaningful for everyone. As we indicated in Chapter 1, being guided by an ideal does not mean that the leadership practice that follows is unrealistic. We hope the book has shown how collaborative leadership is not only challenging but also a creative, inspiring and feasible way of advancing learning in its best and fullest sense.

References

Anderson, E., Barnett, P., Thompson, L., Roberts, A. and Wearing, V. (2014) Teachers are doing it for themselves: knowledge-building in HertsCam, in D. Frost (ed.) *Transforming Education through Teacher Leadership*. Cambridge: Leadership for Learning.

Anderson, S.E., Moore, S. and Sun, J. (2009) Positioning the principals in patterns of school leadership distribution, in K. Leithwood, B. Mascall and T. Strauss, *Distributed Leadership According to the Evidence*. Abingdon: Routledge.

Archer, M.S. (1995) *Realist Social Theory: The Morphogenetic Approach*. Cambridge: Cambridge University Press.

Archer, M.S. (2000) *Being Human: The Problem of Agency*. Cambridge: Cambridge University Press.

Archer, M.S. (2003) *Structure, Agency and the Internal Conversation*. Cambridge: Cambridge University Press.

Archer, M.S. (2012) *The Reflexive Imperative in Late Modernity*. Cambridge: Cambridge University Press.

Arnott, M. and Ozga, J. (2016) Education and nationalism in Scotland: Governing a 'learning nation', *Oxford Review of Education*, 42(3): 253–265.

Aspelin, J. (2014) Beyond individualised teaching: A relational construction of pedagogical attitude, *Education Inquiry*, 5(2): 233–245. Available at: www.education-inquiry.net/index.php/edui/article/view/2392 (accessed 22 July 2017).

Baggini, J. (2015) *Freedom Regained: The Possibility of Free Will*. London: Granta.

Ball, S.J. (2006) Introduction: The problem of policy, in S.J. Ball, *Education Policy and Social Class: The Selected Works of Stephen J. Ball*. London: Routledge. pp. 1–6.

Bates, A. (2016) *Transforming Education: Meanings, Myths and Complexity*. London: Routledge.

Bennett, N., Wise, C., Woods, P.A. and Harvey, J.A. (2003) *Distributed Leadership*. Nottingham: National College for School Leadership.

Berkovich, I. and Eyal, O. (2015) Educational leaders and emotions: An international review of empirical evidence 1992–2012, *Review of Educational Research*, 85(1): 129–167.

Berkovich, I. and Eyal, O. (2017) Emotional reframing as a mediator of the relationships between transformational school leadership and teachers' motivation and commitment, *Journal of Educational Administration*, 55(5): 450–568.

Bhaskar, R. (2010) *Reclaiming Reality: A Critical Introduction to Contemporary Philosophy*. London: Routledge.

Biesta, G. (2009) Good education in an age of measurement: On the need to reconnect with the question of purpose in education, *Educational Assessment, Evaluation and Accountability*, 21(1): 33–46.

Blackmore, J. (1999) *Troubling Women*. Buckinghamshire: Open University Press.

Bolam, R., McMahon, A., Stoll, L., Thomas, S. and Wallace, M. with Greenwood, A., Hawkey, K., Ingram, M., Atkinson, A. and Smith, M. (2005) *Creating and Sustaining Effective Professional Learning Communities*. London: DfES.

Bolden, R. (2011) Distributed leadership in organizations: A review of theory and research, *International Journal of Management Reviews*, 13: 251–269.

Bolden, R., Jones, S., Davis, H. and Gentle, P. (2015) *Developing and Sustaining Shared Leadership in Higher Education*. London: Leadership Foundation for Higher Education.

Boulton, J.G., Allen, P.M. and Bowman, C. (2015) *Embracing Complexity: Strategic Perspectives for an Age of Turbulence*. Oxford: Oxford University Press.

Bradley-Levine, J. and Mosier, G. (2017) Examination of the new tech model as holistic democracy, *Democracy and Education*, 25(1).

Brubaker, R. and Cooper, F. (2000) Beyond identity, *Theory and Society*, 29(1): 1–47.

Burns, J.M. (1978) *Leadership*. New York: Harper and Row.

Bush, T. (2010) Leadership development, in T. Bush, L. Bell and D. Middlewood (eds) *The Principles of Educational Leadership & Management*. London: SAGE.

Bustard, G. (2012) Turning reluctant boys into published writers, *Teacher Leadership*, 3(1): 5–7.

Butler, J. and Athanasiou, A. (2013) *Dispossession: The Performative in the Political*. Cambridge: Polity Press.

Caldwell, R. (2006) *Agency and Change: Rethinking Change Agency in Organisations*. London: Routledge.

Caldwell, R. (2007) Agency and change: Re-evaluating Foucault's legacy, *Organization*, 14(6): 769–791.

Cameron, D.H., Gauthier, G., Ryerson, R. and Kokis, J. (2011) Teacher professional learning from the 'inside out': Studying the student experience as means to teacher action and new knowledge. Paper for submission to peer reviewed journal, Ontario Ministry of Education, Canada.

Capper, C.A. and Young, M. (2014) Ironies and limitations of educational leadership for social justice: A call to social justice educators, *Theory into Practice*, 53: 158–164.

Carr, D. (2011) Values, virtues and professional development in education and teaching, *International Journal of Educational Research*, 50: 171–176.

Carroll, B. (2015) Leadership learning and development, in B. Carroll, J. Ford and S. Taylor (eds) *Leadership*. London: SAGE.

Carroll, B. (2016) Leadership as identity: A practice-based exploration, in J. Raelin (ed.) *Leadership-as-Practice: Theory and Application*. London: Routledge.

Carroll, B., Levy, L. and Richmond, D. (2008) Leadership as practice: Challenging the competency paradigm, *Leadership*, 4(4): 363–379.

Chesborough, H. (2006) Open innovation: A new paradigm for understanding industrial innovation, in H. Chesbrough, W. Vanhaverbeke and J. West (eds) *Open Innovation: Researching a New Paradigm*. Oxford: Oxford University Press.

Collison, C. and Parcell, G. (2004) *Learning to Fly*. Sussex: Capstone.

Cornelissen, J.P. and Werner, M.D. (2014) Putting framing in perspective: A review of framing and frame analysis across the management and organizational literature, *The Academy of Management Annals*, 8(1): 181–223.

Cribb, A. and Gewirtz, S. (2003) Towards a sociology of just practices: An analysis of plural conceptions of justice, in C. Vincent (ed.) *Social Justice, Education and Identity*. London: Routledge-Falmer.

Dallmayr, F. (2007) *In Search of the Good Life*. Lexington: University Press of Kentucky.

Dallmayr, F. (2016) *Freedom and Solidarity*. Lexington: University Press of Kentucky.

Day, C., Sammons, P., Hopkins, D., Harris A., Leithwood, K., Gu, Q., Brown, E., Ahtaridou, E. and Kington, A. (2009) *The Impact of School Leadership on Pupil*

Outcomes: Final Report, Research Report DCSF-RR108. London: Department for Children, Schools and Families.

DeFlaminis, J.A., Abdul-Jabbar, M. and Yoak, E. (2016) *Distributed Leadership in Schools.* London: Routledge.

Denyer, D. and Turnbull James, K. (2016) Doing leadership-as-practice, in J. Raelin (ed.) *Leadership-as-Practice: Theory and Application.* London: Routledge.

Drew, V., Priestley, M. and Michael, M.K. (2016) Curriculum development through critical collaborative professional enquiry, *Journal of Professional Capital and Community,* 1(1): 92–106.

Duif, T., Harrison, C., van Dartel, N. and Sinyolo, D. (2013) *Distributed Leadership in Practice: A Descriptive Analysis of Distributed Leadership in European Schools.* European School Heads Association and European Trade Union Committee for Education, for the European Policy Network on School Leadership.

Earley, P., Higham, R., Allen, R., Allen, T., Howson, J., Nelson, R., Rawar, S., Lynch, S., Morton, L., Mehta, P. and Sims, D. (2012) *Review of the School Leadership Landscape.* Nottingham: National College for School Leadership.

Eddolls, T. (2014) *Hypnofacts 2.* Chippenham: iTech-Ed Hypnotherapy.

Eherensal, P. (2016) The limits of a single candle, in S.J. Gross and J.P Shapiro (eds) *Democratic Ethical Educational Leadership: Reclaiming School Reform.* New York and London: Routledge.

Eltemamy, A. (2017) Establishing a teacher leadership programme in Egypt, in D. Frost (ed.) *Empowering Teachers as Agents of Change: A Non-positional Approach to Teacher Leadership.* Cambridge: Leadership for Learning.

Engeström, Y. (2004) New forms of learning in co-configuration work, *Journal of Workplace Learning,* 16(1/2): 11–21.

Erikson, E. (1975) 'Identity crisis' in Autobiographic perspective, in E. Erikson (ed.) *Life History and the Historical Moment.* New York: Norton.

Fielding, M. (2009) Public space and educational leadership: Reclaiming and renewing our radical traditions, *Educational Management Administration and Leadership,* 37(4): 497–521.

Fielding, M. and Moss, P. (2011) *Radical Education and the Common School.* London: Routledge.

Fielding, M., Bragg, S., Cunningham, I., Erault, M., Horne, M., Robinson, C. and Thorpe, J. (2005) *Factors Affecting the Transfer of Good Practice,* Research Report RR615. London: DfES.

Fink, D. (2005) *Leadership for Mortals: Developing and Sustaining Leaders of Learning.* London: Paul Chapman Publishing.

Fitzgerald, L., Ferlie, E., McGivern, G. and Buchanan, D. (2013) Distributed leadership patterns and service improvement: Evidence and argument from English healthcare, *The Leadership Quarterly,* 24(1): 227–239.

Flinn, K. and Mowles, C. (2014) *A Complexity Approach to Leadership Development: Developing Practical Judgement.* London: Leadership Foundation for Higher Education.

Frost, D. (2006) The concept of 'agency' in leadership for learning, *Leading and Managing,* 12(2): 19–28.

Frost, D. (2008) Teacher leadership: values and voice, *School Leadership and Management,* 28(4): 337–352.

Frost, D. (2011) *Supporting Teacher Leadership in 15 Countries: International Teacher Leadership Project, Phase 1 – A Report.* Cambridge: University of Cambridge Faculty of Education.

Frost, D. (ed.) (2016) *HertsCam Annual Conference 2015: Report.* HertsCam Network. Available at: www.hertscam.ork.uk.

Frost, D. and MacBeath, J. with Stenton, S., Frost, R., Roberts, A. and Wearing, V. (2010) *Learning to Lead: An Evaluation.* Cambridge: Leadership for Learning, University of Cambridge Faculty of Education.

Frost, D. and Roberts, A. with Barnett, P., Bullen, A., Herbert, C., Chiriac, M., Murphy, T., Brace, S., Campbell, L., Impey, C. and Montgomery, C. (2009) *Teacher Leadership in Action.* Paper presented at the 33rd Collaborative Action Research Network International Conference Campus of Athens College/Psychico College Athens, Greece, 30 October–1 November.

Frost, D. and Roberts, A. (2011) Student leadership, participation and democracy, *Leading and Managing,* 17(2): 64–84.

Frost, D., MacBeath, J., Swaffield, S. and Waterhouse, J. (2008) The legacy of the Carpe Vitam Leadership for Learning Project, *inFORM,* 8, Faculty of Education, University of Cambridge.

Gherardi, S. (2016) To start practice theorizing anew: The contribution of the concepts of agencement and formativeness, *Organization,* 23(5): 680–698.

Gibb, C.A. (1968) Leadership, in G. Lindzey and E. Aronson (eds) *The Handbook of Social Psychology, Volume IV,* 2nd edn. Reading, MA: Addison-Wesley. pp. 205–282.

Giddens, A. (1994) *From Beyond Left and Right.* Cambridge: Polity Press.

Gidley, M.G. (2016) *Postformal Education: A Philosophy for Complex Futures.* Basel, Switzerland: Springer International.

Gidley, M.G. (2017) *The Future: A Very Short Introduction.* Oxford: OUP.

Goffman, E. (1959) *The Presentation of Self in Everyday Life.* New York: Doubleday.

Gratton, L. (2004) *The Democratic Enterprise.* London: FT Prentice Hall.

Gratton, L. (2007) *Hot Spots.* Harlow: Pearson Education.

Gratton, L. (2011) *The Shift: The Future of Work is Already Here.* London: HarperCollins.

Gray, J., Kruse, S. and Tarter, C.J. (2016) Enabling school structures, collegial trust and academic emphasis: Antecedents of professional learning communities, *Educational Management Administration and Leadership,* 44(6): 875–891.

Griffin, D. (2002) *The Emergence of Leadership: Linking Self-organization and Ethics.* London: Routledge.

Gronn, P. (2002) Distributed leadership as a unit of analysis, *Leadership Quarterly,* 13(4): 423–451.

Gronn, P. (2003) *The New Work of Educational Leaders.* London: SAGE.

Gronn, P. (2009) Leadership configurations, *Leadership,* 5(3): 381–394.

Gronn, P. (2016) Fit for purpose no more? *Management in Education,* 30(4): 168–172.

Hall, D.J., Gunter, H. and Bragg, J. (2013) The strange case of the emergence of distributed leadership in schools in England, *Educational Review,* 65(4): 467–487.

Hallgarten, J., Hannon, V. and Beresford, T. (2016) *Creative Public Leadership: How School System Leaders Can Create the Conditions for System-wide Innovation.* London: RSA.

Hammersley-Fletcher, L. and Strain, M. (2011) Power, agency and middle leadership in English primary schools, *British Educational Research Journal,* 37(5): 871–884.

Harris, A. (2012) Distributed leadership: Implications for the role of the principal, *Journal of Management Development,* 31(4): 7–17.

Harris, A. and DeFlaminis, J. (2016) Distributed leadership in practice: Evidence, misconceptions and possibilities, *Management in Education,* 30(4): 141–146.

Harris, A. and Lambert, L. (2003) *Building Leadership Capacity for School Improvement.* Maidenhead: Open University Press.

Hartley, D. (2009) Education policy, distributed leadership and socio-cultural theory, *Educational Review*, 61(2): 139–150.

Hawkins, M. and James, C. (2017) Developing a perspective on schools as complex, evolving, loosely linking systems, *Educational Management Administration & Leadership*, published online at DOI: 10.1177/1741143217711192.

Heck, R.H. and Hallinger, P. (2010) Testing a longitudinal model of distributed leadership effects on school improvement, *The Leadership Quarterly*, 21: 867–885.

HertsCam Network (2011) *HertsCam Voice*, special issue on impact, HertsCam Network, 15, March.

Hill, V. (2014) The HertsCam TLDW programme, in D. Frost (ed.) *Transforming Education through Teacher Leadership*. Cambridge: Leadership for Learning/The Cambridge Network.

Hitlin, S. (2003) Values as the core of personal identity: Drawing links between two theories of self, *Social Psychology Quarterly*, 66(2): 118–137.

Holden, G. (2008) Knowledge-building and networking: The Leadership for Learning case, *School Leadership and Management*, 28(4): 307–322.

Holmwood, J. (2014) Reflexivity as situated problem-solving: A pragmatist alternative to general theory, *Sociologica*, 1: 1–26.

James, W. (2004) Does 'consciousness' exist? *Journal of Philosophy, Psychology, and Scientific Methods*, 1: 477–491.

Jeffrey, B. and Troman, G. (2012a) The performative institutional embrace, *Journal of Organizational Ethnography*, 1(2): 195–212.

Jeffrey, B. and Troman, G. (eds) (2012b) *Performativity in UK Education: Ethnographic Cases of its Effects, Agency and Reconstructions*. Stroud: EandE Publishing.

Jeffrey, B. and Troman, G. (2014) The construction of performative identities, in A. Rasmussen, J. Gustafsson and B. Jeffrey (eds) *Performativity in Education: An International Collection of Ethnographic Research on Learners' Experiences*. Stroud: EandE Publishing.

Jenkins, R. (1996) *Social Identity*. London: Routledge.

Jones, S. (2015) Contrived collegiality? Investigating the efficacy of co-operative teacher development, in T. Woodin (ed.) *Co-operation, Learning and Co-operative Values*. London: Routledge.

Kensler, L.A.W. (2008) *The Ecology of Democratic Learning Communities*, unpublished PhD thesis, Bethlehem, PA, US: Lehigh University.

Kensler, L.A.W. and Uline, C.L. (2017) *Leadership for Green Schools: Sustainability for Our Children, Our Communities, and Our Planet*. New York: Routledge.

Klar, H.W., Huggins, K.S., Hammonds, H.L. and Buskey, F.C. (2016) Fostering the capacity for distributed leadership: A post-heroic approach to leading school improvement, *International Journal of Leadership in Education*, 19(2): 111–137.

Kollias, A. and Hatzopoulos, P. (eds) (2013) *School Leadership Policy Development: The EPNoSL Briefing Notes*. European Policy Network on School Leadership. Available at: www.schoolleadership.eu/portal/deliverable/briefing-notes-school-leadership-policy-development (accessed 8 January 2015).

Kools, M. and Stoll, L. (2016) *What Makes a School a Learning Organisation?* OECD Education Working Papers 137. Paris: OECD Publishing. Available at: http://dx.doi.org/10.1787/5jlwm62b3bvh-en.

Ladkin, D. (2010) *Rethinking Leadership: A New Look at Old Leadership Questions*, Cheltenham: Edward Elgar.

Leithwood, K. and Mascall, B. (2008) Collective leadership effects on student achievement, *Educational Administration Quarterly*, 44(4): 529–561.

Leithwood, K., Day, C., Sammons, P., Harris, A. and Hopkins, D. (2006) *Successful School Leadership: What it is and How it Influences Pupil Learning*, Research Report RR800. London: Department for Education and Skills.

Levin, B. (2003) *Approaches to Equity in Policy for Lifelong Learning*. Paris: OECD.

Lingard, B., Hayes, D., Mills, M. and Christie, P. (2003) *Leading Learning*. Maidenhead: Open University Press.

Louis, K.S., Leithwood, K., Wahlstrom, K.L. and Anderson, S.E. (2010) *Investigating the Links to Improved Student Learning: Final Report of Research Findings*. St Paul, MN: University of Minnesota.

Lumby, J. (2013) Distributed leadership: The uses and abuses of power, *Educational Management Administration and Leadership*, 41(5): 581–597.

Lumby, J. (2016) Distributed leadership as fashion or fad, *Management in Education*, 30(4): 161–167.

Lumby, J. and Coleman, M. (2016) *Leading for Equality: Making Schools Fairer*. London: SAGE.

Martin, G.P. and Learmouth, M. (2012) A critical account of the rise and spread of 'leadership': The case of UK healthcare, *Social Science and Medicine*, 74(3): 281–288.

McElroy, M.W. (2010) *The New Knowledge Management: Complexity, Learning and Sustainable Innovation*. London: Routledge.

Miettinen, R. (2013) *Innovation, Human Capabilities and Democracy*. Oxford: Oxford University Press.

Moore, J.W. (2016) What is the sense of agency and why does it matter? *Frontiers in Psychology*, 29 August. DOI: 10.3389/fpsyg.2016.01272.

Mylles, J. (2017) Building a school culture through scholarship: A long-term strategy, in D. Frost (ed.) *Empowering Teachers as Agents of Change: A Non-positional Approach to Teacher Leadership*. Cambridge: Leadership for Learning.

National College for School Leadership (2004) *Distributed Leadership: Action Pack*. Nottingham: National College for School Leadership.

Noordegraaf, M. and Schinkel, W. (2011) Professional capital contested: A bourdieusian analysis of conflicts between professionals and managers, *Comparative Sociology*, 10: 97–125.

Norton, D.L. (1996) *Democracy and Moral Development: A Politics of Virtue*. Berkeley, CA: University of California Press.

Norton-Taylor, V. and Lightfoot, S. (2017) Developing the role of atelierista, in D. Frost (ed.) *Empowering Teachers as Agents of Change: A Non-positional Approach to Teacher Leadership*. Cambridge: Leadership for Learning.

OECD (2013) *Innovative Learning Environments, Educational Research and Innovation*. Paris: OECD Publishing.

Osborne, S.P., Radnor, Z. and Nasi, G. (2013) A new theory for public service management? Toward a (public) service-dominant, *American Review of Public Administration*, 43(2): 135–158.

Osler, A. and Starkey, H. (2006) Education for democratic citizenship: A review of research, policy and practice 1995–2005, *Research Papers in Education*, 21(4): 433–466.

Oyediwura, M. and Gaiteri, T. (2017) A project to develop children's character through the teaching and modelling of virtues, in D. Frost (ed.) *Empowering Teachers as Agents of Change: A Non-positional Approach to Teacher Leadership*. Cambridge: Leadership for Learning/The Cambridge Network.

Perkins, D. (2003) *Making Thinking Visible*. Available at: http://www.visiblethinkingpz. org/VisibleThinking_html_files/06_AdditionalResources/MakingThinkingVisible_ DP.pdf (accessed 13 December 2017).

Peters, M.A. and Heraud, R. (2015) Toward a political theory of social innovation: Collective intelligence and the co-creation of social goods, *Journal of Self-Governance and Management Economics*, 3(3): 7–23.

Polanyi, M. (1966) *The Tacit Dimension*. London: Routledge and Kegan Paul.

Puonti, A. (2004) *Learning to Work Together: Collaboration Between Authorities in Economic-Crime Investigation*. University of Helsinki.

Raelin, J. (2016a) Introduction to leadership-as-practice, in J. Raelin (ed.) *Leadership-as-Practice: Theory and Application*. London: Routledge.

Raelin, J. (ed.) (2016b) *Leadership-as-Practice: Theory and Application*. London: Routledge.

Révai, N. and Guerriero, S. (2017) Knowledge dynamics in the teaching profession, in S. Guerriero (ed.) *Pedagogical Knowledge and the Changing Nature of the Teaching Profession*. Paris: OECD Publishing.

Rhodes, C. and Brundrett, M. (2010) Leadership for learning, in T. Bush, L. Bell and D. Middlewood (eds) *The Principles of Educational Leadership & Management*. London: SAGE.

Roberts, A. (2005) Transposing a culture: Reflections on the leadership of a closing school, *Improving Schools*, 8(3): 237–253.

Roberts, A. (2011) Exploring professional knowledge-building through an inter-school visits programme, *Improving Schools*, 14(1): 15–29.

Roberts, A. and Nash, J. (2009) Enabling students to participate in school improvement through a Students as Researchers programme, *Improving Schools*, 12(2): 184–187.

Roberts, A. and Woods, P.A. (2017) Principles for enhancing teachers' collaborative practice: Lessons from the HertsCam Network, in D. Frost (ed.) *Empowering Teachers as Agents of Change: A Non-positional Approach to Teacher Leadership*. Cambridge: Leadership for Learning.

Roberts, A., Woods, P.A. and Chivers, L. (2017) *Collaborative Teacher Learning: A Summary of Cases from the EFFeCT project*. Hatfield, Hertfordshire: Centre for Educational Leadership, School of Education, University of Hertfordshire. (Further information about the EFFeCT project is available at http://oktataskepzes.tka.hu/en/effect-project.)

Robinson, V.M.J. (2006) Putting education back into educational leadership, *Leading and Managing*, 12(1): 62–75.

Robinson, V.M.J., Lloyd, C.A. and Rowe, K.J. (2008) The impact of leadership on student outcomes: An analysis of the differential effects of leadership types, *Educational Administration Quarterly*, 44(5): 635–674.

Schlappa, H. and Imani, Y. (2012) *Leadership and Structure in the Co-production of Public Services*, University of Hertfordshire Business School Working Paper. Available at: https://uhra.herts.ac.uk/dspace/handle/2299/5549.

Schlappa, H. and Imani, Y. (forthcoming) Who is in the lead? New perspectives on leading service co-production, in T. Steen, B. Verschuere and T. Brandsen Co-*Production and Co-Creation: Engaging Citizens in Public Services*. London: Routledge.

Schwartz, S.H. (2016) Basic individual values: Sources and consequences, in T. Brosch and D. Sander (eds), *Handbook of Value*. Oxford: Oxford University Press.

Scott, P. (1989) Accountability, responsiveness and responsibility in R. Glatter (ed.) *Educational Institutions and their Environments: Managing the Boundaries*. Milton Keynes: Open University Press.

Scott, S. (2010) Revisiting the total institution: Performative regulation in the re-inventive institution, *Sociology*, 44(2): 213–231.

Scribner, S.M.P. and Bradley-Levine, J. (2010) The meaning(s) of teacher leadership in an urban high school reform, *Educational Administration Quarterly*, 46: 491–522.

Seel, R. (2000) Culture and complexity: New insights on organisational change, *Organisations and People*, 7(2): 2–9.

Seel, R. (2006) *Emergence in Organisations*. Available at: www.new-paradigm.co.uk/emergence-2.htm (accessed 3 June 2006).

Sejdini, M. (2014) Building social cohesion through language learning in multi-ethnic Macdeonia, in D. Frost (ed.) *Transforming Education through Teacher Leadership*. Cambridge: Leadership for Learning/The Cambridge Network.

Sen (2009) *The Idea of Justice*. London: Allen Lane.

Simmel, G. (1997) Spatial and urban culture, in D. Frisby and M. Featherstone (eds) *Simmel on Culture*. London: SAGE.

Slavin, R.E. (2010) Co-operative learning: What makes group-work work? in H. Dumont, D. Istance and F. Benavides (eds) *The Nature of Learning*. Paris: OECD. pp. 161–178.

Sorensen, E. (2010) *Governance and Democracy* (Working Paper). Roskilde: Centre for Democratic Network Governance, Roskilde University.

Stacey, R. (2010) *Complexity and Organizational Reality: Uncertainty and the Need to Rethink Management after the Collapse of Investment Capitalism*. Abingdon: Routledge.

Stacey, R. (2012) *Tools and Techniques of Leadership and Management: Meeting the Challenge of Complexity*. London: Routledge.

Stockwell, L., Smith, K. and Woods, P.A. (2017) *That which is Worthy of Love: A Philosophical Investigation of Pedagogic Partnership in Higher Education*. Hatfield: University of Hertfordshire.

Stoll, L. (2011) Leading professional learning communities, in J. Robertson and H.S. Timperley (eds) *Leadership and Learning*. London: SAGE.

Swaffield, S. (2014) Reflecting on themes in teacher leadership using principles of Leadership for Learning, European Conference on Educational Research, Porto, 2–5 September.

Tabberer, R. (2003) *Knowledge and Innovation: 'Five Easy Pieces'*. London: TTA.

Tajfel, H. (1982) Social psychology of intergroup relations, *Annual Review of Psychology*, 33: 1–39.

Taylor, C. (2007) *A Secular Age*. Cambridge, MA and London: Belknap Harvard.

Theoharis, G. and Causton, J. (2014) Leading inclusive reform for students with disabilities: A school- and systemwide approach, *Theory Into Practice*, 53(2): 82–97.

Thorpe, R., Gold, J. and Lawler, J. (2011) Locating distributed leadership, *International Journal of Management Reviews*, 13: 239–250.

Tian, M. (2015) Finnish teachers' perceptions on distributed leadership: Resource and agency, *Contemporary Educational Leadership*, 2(2): 51–74.

Tian, M. (2016) *Distributed Leadership in Finnish and Shanghai Schools*, academic dissertation for PhD, University of Jyväskylä, Finland.

Tian, M., Risku, M. and Collin, K. (2016) A meta-analysis of distributed leadership from 2002 to 2013, *Educational Management Administration and Leadership*, 44(1): 146–164.

Timperley, H.S. and Robertson, R. (2011) Establishing platforms for leadership and learning, in J. Robertson and H.S. Timperley (eds) *Leadership and Learning*. London: SAGE. pp. 3–12.

Torrance, D. (2013) Distributed leadership: Still in the gift of the headteacher, *Scottish Educational Review*, 45(2): 50–63.

Ulhøi, J.P. and Müller, S. (2014) Mapping the landscape of shared leadership: A review and synthesis, *International Journal of Leadership Studies*, 8(2): 66–87.

Uljens, M., Sundqvist, R. and Smeds-Nylund, A. (2016) Educational leadership for sustained multi-level school development in Finland, *Nordic Studies in Education*, 36(2): 103–124.

UNESCO (2015) *Global Citizenship Education: Topics and Learning Objectives*. Paris: UNESCO.

van Hulst, M. and Yanow, D. (2016) From policy 'frames' to 'framing': Theorizing a more dynamic, political approach, *American Review of Public Administration*, 46(1): 92–112.

Vangrieken, K., Dochy, F., Raes, E. and Kyndt, E. (2015) Teacher collaboration: A systematic review, *Educational Research Review*, 15: 17–40.

Vincent, A. and Plant, R. (1984) *Philosophy, Politics and Citizenship*. Oxford: Blackwell.

Von Hippel, E. (2005) *Democratizing Innovation*. Cambridge, MA: The MIT Press.

Wang, D., Waldman, D.A. and Zhang, Z. (2014) A meta-analysis of shared leadership and team effectiveness, *Journal of Applied Psychology*, 99(2): 181–198.

Ward, S.C., Bagley, C., Woods, P.A., Lumby, J., Hamilton, T. and Roberts, A. (2015) School leadership for equity: Lessons from the literature, *International Journal of Inclusive Education*, 19(4): 333–346.

Ward, S.C, Bagley, C., Woods, P.A., Lumby, J., Hamilton, T. and Roberts, A. (2016) What is 'policy' and what is 'policy response'? An illustrative study of the implementation of the Leadership Standards for Social Justice in Scotland, *Educational Management Administration and Leadership*, 44(1): 43–56.

Warmington, P., Daniels, H., Edwards, A., Brown, S., Leadbetter, J., Martin, D. and Middleton, D. (2004) *Interagency Collaboration: A Review of the Literature, the Learning in and for Interagency Working Project*, University of Bath.

Waterhouse, J. (2008) Raising aspirations within school communities: The Learning Catalysts project, *School Leadership and Management*, 28(4): 369–384.

Wearing, V. (2011) *HertsCam: An Evaluation*, commissioned by the HertsCam Steering Committee. Available at: www.hertscam.org.uk/publications (accessed 2 January 2015).

Weber, S.M. (2013) *'The Systemdesigner'– The Rise of a New Academic Transprofession in the Creative University?* Paper presented at the presented at European Conference on Educational Research, Bahçeşehir University, Istanbul, Turkey, 10–13 September.

Wenger, E. (1998) *Communities of Practice*. Cambridge: Cambridge University Press.

Wenger-Trayner, E., Fenton-O'Creevy, M., Hutchinson, S., Kubiak, C. and Wenger-Trayner, B. (2015) *Learning in Landscapes of Practice: Boundaries, Identity, and Knowledgeability in Practice-based Learning*. Abingdon: Routledge.

West, M., Armit, K., Loewenthal, L., Eckert, R., West, T. and Lee, A. (2015) *Leadership and Leadership Development in Healthcare: The Evidence Base*. London: Faculty of Medical Leadership and Management.

Western, S. (2008) *Leadership: A Critical Text*. London: SAGE.

Western, S. (2012) *Coaching and Mentoring: A Critical Text*. London: SAGE.

Western, S. (2013) *Leadership: A Critical Text*, 2nd edn. London: SAGE.

Woods, G.J. and Woods, P.A. (2008) Democracy and spiritual awareness: Interconnections and implications for educational leadership, *International Journal of Children's Spirituality*, 13(2): 101–116.

Woods, G.J. and Woods, P.A. (2013) *Degrees of Democracy Framework: A Review of Its Use and Impact*, Report for School of Education, University of Hertfordshire. Available at:

http://vuh-la-risprt.herts.ac.uk/portal/en/publications/degrees-of-democracy-frame work(ef118220-d05b-4b72-81df-37e8ededf050).html (accessed 2 January 2015).

Woods, P.A. (2005) *Democratic Leadership in Education*. London: SAGE.

Woods, P.A. (2011) *Transforming Education Policy: Shaping a Democratic Future*. Bristol: Policy Press.

Woods, P.A. (2012) *A Four-fold Approach to Social Justice*, information sheet. Available at: www.academia.edu/5755395/A_Four-fold_Approach_to_Social_Justice (accessed 8 January 2015).

Woods, P.A. (2013) Drivers to holistic democracy: Signs and signals of emergent, democratic self-organising systems, in S.M. Weber, M. Göhlich, A. Schröer, H. Macha and C. Fahrenwald (eds) *Organisation und Partizipation: Beiträge der Kommission Organisationspädagogik*. Berlin: Springer VS. pp. 343–356.

Woods, P.A. (2015a) Distributed leadership for equity and learning, *Revista Lusófona de Educação*, 30: 175–187.

Woods, P.A. (2015b) What is democratic leadership?, in D. Griffiths and J. Portelli (eds) *Key Questions for Administrators*. Burlington, Ontario: Word and Deed Publishing.

Woods, P.A. (2016a) Democratic roots: Feeding the multiple dimensions of 'leadership-as-practice', in J. Raelin (ed.) *Leadership-as-Practice: Theory and Application*. London: Routledge.

Woods, P.A. (2016b) Authority, power and distributed leadership, *Management in Education*, 30(4): 155–160.

Woods, P.A. (2017a) Freedom: Uniqueness and diversity at the heart of social justice, in P.S. Angelle (ed.) *A Global Perspective of Social Justice for School Principals*. Charlotte, NC: Information Age Publishing.

Woods, P.A. (2017b) Researching holistic democracy in schools, *Democracy and Education*, 25(1).

Woods, P.A. and Gronn, P. (2009) Nurturing democracy: The contribution of distributed leadership to a democratic organisational landscape, *Educational Management Administration and Leadership*, 37(4): 430–451.

Woods, P.A. and Roberts, A. (2013a) *Distributed Leadership and Social Justice (DLSJ): National Review*, prepared for European Policy Network on School Leadership. Available at: https://herts.academia.edu/PhilipWoods (accessed 2 January 2015).

Woods, P.A. and Roberts, A. (2013b) *Distributed Leadership and Social Justice: A Case Study Investigation of Distributed Leadership and the Extent to which it Promotes Social Justice and Democratic Practices*, full report with appendices. Available under 'Reports and Papers' at: https://herts.academia.edu/PhilipWoods (accessed 2 January 2015).

Woods, P.A. and Roberts, A. (2015) *Developing Distributed Leadership for Equity and Learning: A Toolset for Policy-makers and School Leaders*, European Policy Network on School Leadership (EPNoSL). Available at: https://herts.academia.edu/PhilipWoods (accessed 2 January 2016).

Woods, P.A. and Roberts, A. (2016) Distributed leadership and social justice: Images and meanings from different positions across the school landscape, *International Journal of Leadership in Education*, 19(2): 138–156.

Woods, P.A. and Woods, G.J. (2012) Degrees of school democracy: A holistic framework, *Journal of School Leadership*, 22(4): 707–732.

Woods, P.A. and Woods, G.J. (2013) Deepening distributed leadership: A democratic perspective on power, purpose and the concept of the self, *Leadership in Education (Vodenje v vzgoji in izobraževanju)*, 2: 17–40. An English language version is available to download under 'Journal Articles' at: https://herts.academia.edu/PhilipWoods.

Woods, P.A., Bagley, C. and Glatter, R. (1998) *School Choice and Competition: Markets in the Public Interest*. London: Routledge.

Woods, P.A., Bennett, N., Harvey, J.A. and Wise, C. (2004) Variabilities and dualities in distributed leadership: Findings from a systematic literature review, *Educational Management Administration and Leadership*, 32(4): 439–457.

Woods, P.A., Roberts, A. and Chivers, L. (2016) *Collaborative Teacher Learning: Cases from the HertsCam Network*. Hatfield, Hertfordshire: Centre for Educational Leadership, School of Education, University of Hertfordshire.

Wren, J.T. (1998) James Madison and the ethics of transformational leadership, in J.B. Ciulla (ed.) *Ethics: The Heart of Leadership*. Westport, CN: Praeger.

Index

co-operative professional development 92
co-production 22
coaching 102
coercive persuasion 75–6
cognitive frame 119
cognitive reframing 120
collaborative culture 19
collaborative leadership x
  authorisation 110–11
  challenges of complexity for 107–10
  communities of leadership practice 82–3
  concepts and messiness 73
  conceptualisation x, 12, 47–8
  creative spaces 100–4
  democratic citizenship and 25
  enabling structures 96–100
  identity change 116–24
  inclusion 25
  leadership development from across the
      school 23, 68, 81, 82, 99, 111–13
  multiple authorities 79–81, 110–11
  pro-active agency 65
  reciprocal learning 74–9
  as a transformational process 86–7
  value-base 27, 43
  see also emergence; identity;
      intentionality; philosophy of
      co-development
collaborative leadership learning groups
    (CLLGs) 90–1
collaborative learning 21, 25, 28, 62, 81,
    88–92, 127, 131
collaborative professional networks 23
collective identity construction 121–3
collegiality 99
communicative reflexivity 66
communicative virtues 121
communities 63
communities of leadership
    practice 100, 113
  authorisations 83, 114, 115
  diverse intentionalities in schools 82–3
  intentionalities and initiatives 82
  social justice 113, 114
complexity
  appreciating 107
  challenges for developing collaborative
      leadership 107–10
  power and 56
complexity theory 4, 5, 6, 8, 14–15, 36,
    43, 56
  connectivity 89
  emergent systems 51
  idealising leaders 75
  leadership development 87

organisational life and 50, 53
senior leaders and 107
connectivity 89
Contemplation Pods 103
contractual exchange 44–5
Cornelissen, Joep and Werner, Mirjam 42
Cornelissen, J.P. and Werner, M.D. 119
corporate teams 35
creative spaces 100–4
  agency space 101
  physical and socially created spaces 103
  subjective space 101–2, 104
  thinking spaces 102
  trialectic space 101
Cribb, Alan and Gewirtz, Sharon 64
Critical Collaborative Professional Enquiry
    (CCPE) programme 91, 93
critical intentionality 49, 56, 64–71, 77–8, 102
  subjectification 68
critical reflection 79
critical reflexivity 50, 63, 65, 67, 69,
    76, 88, 102
  characterisation of 69
  values framework 71–2
critical research 32, 34, 36
critical thinking 75, 76
cultural justice 64, 70, 109
culture
  applied distributed leadership 51–2
  cohesive 26–7, 30
  collaborative 19, 112
  definition 96
  headteachers building of 108, 109, 112
  participatory 96–7, 100
  in schools 52

Day et al. 17, 17n2, 18, 19, 27
deep learning 25, 36, 38, 72
DeFlaminis et al. 19
DeMo project 70
democratic authority 80, 110, 113
democratic citizenship 24–5
democratic innovation 21–2
democratic leadership 3, 4, 27, 63, 129
democratic logic 44–5
Denyer, David and James, Kim Turnbull 119
developmental democracy 62
developmental injustice 68
developmental justice 64
dialogue 76, 111
  transforming 131
disciplinary power 75, 76
discourses
  of leadership 59
  organisational 96–7

HertsCam Network 26, 28, 78, 91, 93, 98, 108
  Annual Conference 122–3
  collective construction of identity 122
  values clarification 118
hierarchical leadership 3–4, 8
  discourses of 59
  fluid nature of 52
  see also top-down hierarchical leadership
Hill, Val 122–3
holistic democracy ix, x, 58–9, 62–3, 72, 96, 129–30
  collaborative learning 62
  core purpose of 127
  critical questions on 123–4
  definition 126
  holistic learning 62, 63
  intellectual roots of 62
  notion of 11
  power sharing 63
  purpose of 62
  relational well-being 62, 63
  transforming dialogue 63
holistic growth 16, 62, 64, 72, 96, 127
  as a relational process 62
holistic learning 62, 63, 131
hot spots 54, 66, 89
human growth 38, 78
hybrid leadership 6

ideas 97
  key, interconnection of 125–7
identification 117, 122
identity
  as an active process 117
  collective identity construction 121–3
  definitions 116–17
  as fixed 116–17
  nurturing key capabilities 120–1
  as a process of development 117
  reframing leadership 119–20
  values and 117
  values clarification 118–19
improvement capacity 18
inclusive participation 71–2, 96, 127
independent zones 103
individual-social dualism 55
individualistic behaviour 21
inequalities 32, 72
  organisational and social boundaries 40
  of power 52
  in social justice 23, 64
  social positioning 39–40
  socio-economic 64

initiation 67, 76, 77, 81
innovation 21–3, 66, 90, 100
  co-production 22
  collaborative interaction 21, 22
  democratic/distributed 21–2
  distributed 21–2
  open 22, 23
  social 22, 23
innovative emergence 90
Innovative Experience Schools (IESs) 53
Inset (in-service professional training) 108
institutional architecture 97–8, 100
instrumental learning 131
instrumental rationality 32, 34, 36
intellectual virtues 10n7
intentionality ix, 7, 8–9, 48–50
  communities of leadership practice 82
  definition 48, 126
  expression of 48
  individual and group-led 113
  knowledge creation 56
  occurrences of 49
  ontological status of the individual 55
  recognition of 48, 49–50
  relationship with emergence 54–7
  variables relating to 49
  see also critical intentionality; emergence
internal conversations 102
international assessments 16
International Teacher Leadership project 112
interplays 100

Jeffrey, Bob and Troman, Geoff 34–5
Jones, Sarah 92, 99, 100, 121–2

Kensler, Lisa and Uline, Cynthia 60
knowing in practice 86–8, 91, 92
knowledge 56
  creation of 56, 86
  explicit 88
  practice and 56–7, 87
  reciprocal learning and 78
  tacit 88
knowledge management 89

Ladkin, Donna 4, 119
landscape of leadership practice 82–3, 84, 106–14
Latvia 53
lead agency 109–10
leadership 6–7
  basic nature of 126

social dynamics 94, 95
social environments 99
social freedom 69
social identity 117
social innovation 22, 23
social justice ix, x, 2, 55, 58–9, 72, 96, 102
   critical questions on 113–14
   and distributed leadership 61
   four-fold scheme 64, 113
   inequalities in 23, 64
   notion of 11
   open innovation and 23
   values of 61
social life 8
social positioning 39–40
social processes 94
social spaces 103
social structures 8, 9
socialisation 68
soft accountability 28
spectrum of possibilities 55
Spillane, Jim 55
Stacey, Ralph 7, 75, 107, 120–1
standards and accountability agenda 16
status availability 121
structure(s) 8, 9, 94, 101
   trialectic process 94, 95, 101
   see also enabling structures
student leadership 27
students, relationship with teachers 76
subjectification 68
subjective space 101–2, 104
superhero/collaborative leadership 55

Tabberer, R. 89
tacit knowledge 88
Tajfel, H. 117
targets 36
Taylor, Charles 4
teacher collaboration 19
teacher leadership 67, 108, 111, 112
   development projects 43
Teacher Led Development Work (TLDW)
   Groups 22, 28, 65, 78,
   79, 91, 98
teacher-led projects 78–9, 91
teachers
   collaborative development work 108
   cooperative interactions 53
   good practice 88
   identity construction 122
   as leaders 33
   relationship with headteachers 76
   relationship with students 76
   stories of change 122

thinking routine 88–9
   see also networks/networking
TEAM approach 35
teams 34–5
techniques of power 75
tests/testing 37–8
   see also SATs (Standard Assessment Tasks)
thinking routine 88–9
thinking spaces 102
Tian et al. 16, 55
TLRs (Teaching and Learning Responsibility
   payments) 18
top-down hierarchical leadership 4, 5, 39,
   41, 42, 52
   authority and 79
   emotions 119–20
   flow 3–4
   fluidity in organisations 52
Torrance, D. 109
traditional authority 80, 110, 113
traditional reflexivity 66, 67
training 27, 28, 80, 81, 107, 108, 110
   Inset (in-service professional training) 108
transformational leadership 77
transforming dialogue 63
transmission model of developing leadership
   change 85–6, 92
trialectic space 101
trialectic view of social dynamics 94, 95,
   99, 101
trust 26, 27, 109
truth 63

Uljens, Michael 76
UNESCO 24
University of Limerick (UL) 81
utility-based relationship 9–10

value-bases 2, 9, 25, 43, 127
   holistic democracy 102
   leadership practice 32, 43, 126
   philosophy of co-development 12, 27, 32,
   43, 45, 49, 60, 96, 118, 127
   philosophy of dependence 127
   social justice 102
values 9, 10, 43
   clarification 43, 117, 118–19, 123,
   127, 128
   in eco-leadership 60
   elaboration of 59–62
   framework to aid critical reflexivity 71–2
   in identity 117
   of social justice 61
   values clarification 124
   see also holistic democracy; social justice